This is a beautiful book, that made me laugh out loud and cry. This is more than a story about a mischievous bird. It's about a young couple who learned about love, parenting, and each other through and unlikely character.

Lisa Fabrizio: Director and Professor of Massage Therapy
and Healing Arts: Spanish Fort, Alabama

One of the most fascinating and heartwarming books I have ever read. The story becomes alive to me. A sequel should be written.

Calvin Patterson CPA:
CFO Financial Consulting Services: Marietta, Georgia

Edgar & Susan

The Crow and the Woman He Loved

MOSES PATE

WESTBOW·
PRESS
A DIVISION OF THOMAS NELSON
& ZONDERVAN

WestBow Press books may be ordered through booksellers or by contacting:

WestBow Press
A Division of Thomas Nelson & Zondervan
1663 Liberty Drive
Bloomington, IN 47403
www.westbowpress.com
1 (866) 928-1240

ISBN: 978-1-4908-2696-7 (sc)
ISBN: 978-1-4908-2697-4 (hc)
ISBN: 978-1-4908-2695-0 (e)

Library of Congress Control Number: 2014903094

Printed in the United States of America.

WestBow Press rev. date: 02/19/2014

CONTENTS

DEDICATION

It pleases me to dedicate this story to a lady who changed the direction of my life. My second-grade schoolteacher, Mrs. Wallace, was one of those dedicated and caring educators who understand that their profession is a calling and a mission. I believe that every schoolteacher, just like every minister, Sunday school teacher, coach, or even technical instructor, desires to know that at least one child has been positively affected by their instruction. I now tell Mrs. Wallace that I am her child.

Mrs. Wallace taught the second grade at Forest Hill Elementary School in Mobile, Alabama, during the 1961–1962 session. I entered her classroom in fear and trepidation, because I had left the first grade angered and disillusioned. Early in the first grade, I developed painful ear problems, which adversely affected my ability to hear my teacher and understand my lessons. I was assigned a seat at the "dummy table." The "normal" kids helped to reinforce my opinion that I was stupid. "Red on the head and stupid" became my identity. Kids can be cruel. Somehow I squeaked out a promotion to the second grade.

Mrs. Wallace escorted her class to the school library every Tuesday morning. She apparently noticed that I would always choose the simplest book I could find. Dr. Seuss books were my favorites. I couldn't read them, but I enjoyed the pictures. One day she took me aside, knelt down in front of me, and compassionately looked at me through her horn-rimmed glasses.

She said so sweetly, "I know something you don't know." Then she continued, "You're a very smart boy, but you don't know it yet." She went on to explain that I needed to pick out some books on a higher reading level. She looked through the shelves and brought me a book titled *The White Panther*. Mrs. Wallace told me to ask her for help anytime I needed it, which I did eagerly and often. She was always loving and patient.

For every child, somewhere there is a certain book that will open the wonderful world of reading to them. With Mrs. Wallace's help, I learned to read and devour books. She helped me to be carried away into worlds that I had never dreamed of. I have never read a book without thinking of this wonderful lady.

Thank you, Mrs. Wallace. You've earned your special reward in heaven.

> Whosoever shall receive one of such children in my name, receiveth me: and whosoever shall receive me, receiveth not me, but him that sent me.
>
> —Mark 9:37 KJV

ACKNOWLEDGEMENTS

I am grateful to friends and family that helped me with this narrative about our old friend Edgar. Each one has their own special story about him.

Thanks for the opportunity to share some good laughs about some great memories. Great memories, shared by good old friends, have a value beyond price.

Thanks to Tony Smith, Mickey Dodd, Philip Brooks and our late dear friend Buck McLeod for your unconditional friendship. Thanks to my brother Richard. You lived this story with me.

Here's to you, my brother Sammy, for your keen insights and thought provoking perspectives. Russell, my late beloved brother, always saw the good, and encouraged me in everything I ever did.

Thanks to my children, Daniel, Ab, Luke, and Allison for your persistence in asking me to write this book. A very special nod goes to Luke, and my daughter in law Cristie, for your patience and help in putting this book together.

Thanks most of all to my precious wife Susan. When we first met, I told myself that if I could have you for my wife, I would be happy for the rest of my life. I was right! I am one of those fortunate men that found the one girl in the whole world that God meant for him. To this day, every morning when I see you, I am more in love with you than I was in the long ago beginning.

INTRODUCTION

My children and their children have always heard various incredible stories and references about a crow named Edgar. My wife, Susan, and I would jokingly refer to him as "our first child." Many times while relating anecdotes about Edgar, they would realize that their own little quirks and actions were being compared to a crow. We've enjoyed a lot of laughter during most of these "comparisons"; however, when used in the context of corrections, they sometimes showed signs of annoyance at my pointing out the similarities they shared with a bird.

They just didn't understand, and later, they always went to Susan to check out the accuracy or even the suspected embellishments of the stories. She would listen with amusement before confirming the accounts. Susan was often able to add her own perspectives to the incident in question. Her ability to tell the same story gave it the stamp of the "gospel truth."

They asked me many times to sit down and write an account of the unusual story of Edgar. I've lived my life in the "throttle wide open" position, which made it hard for me to sit still very long for anything, until one day my daughter and granddaughter put it in another way. They said, "Pappy, will you please write down your memories?" That did it. What else could I do? After dusting off old diaries, journals, and almost indecipherable work reports, and adding the invaluable recollections of Susan, my brothers, and old friends, I began to write down my memories of the story of my friend Edgar.

This is the story of raising children, hidden beneath the story of raising a crow. Susan and I learned many lessons that would later serve us well. At the time, we had no idea that we were gaining valuable knowledge, but later when the kids came along, we realized that the entire crazy experience had indeed served a blessed purpose. I haven't offered any advice, only parallels.

Edgar gave me a deep understanding of how people can truly love a pet, and he also turned me into a fascinated and passionate lover of birds. This is also, and perhaps foremost, a love story—the love that a bird had for a woman, which would eventually become reciprocal, and the love that I have for Susan, which began at first sight and remains eternal.

Love stories are invariably about memories. After nearly four decades, memory can be like trying to look through a fog. Some images seem to lurk behind dark places and behind closed doors that you dare not open, and some seem to illuminate out of the corner of your eye, making you turn to give your full attention. Memory can be like a pleasant old friend. If you're not careful, it can be a horrible enemy. It can give you confidence in situations like dealing with people or suppressing fear. I've had my share of the ones in the dark places, and there are many doors that will remain closed, but I've had far more than my fair share of the bright happy memories that I enjoy turning toward to bask in their warm glow.

Here is what I've always told my children. Pay attention to what goes on around you, because you're always making memories. And be careful what kind you make, because you'll need them when you, too, become old.

I would now like to tell you about some of the memories that will cause me to smile even when death is standing in the doorway. I remember the early springtime of 1976 when Susan told me that we were expecting our first child. I remember being absolutely happy. It was a dream come true, which quickly became a feeling of being stunned. The responsibility was frightening.

Later, I went down in the woods to be alone and pray. I prayed to the Lord that somehow he would do something to give me knowledge and wisdom and prepare me for such an awesome event. I'll not be so presumptuous as to say that God spoke to me, but I will say in all boldness that I gained peace of mind. I immediately turned the corner into the world of solid manhood. I frequently returned to this little place in the woods for solitude and reflection. I would later refer to it as "My Bethel."

EPIGRAPH

Thank you for the days,
Those endless days, those sacred days you gave me.
I'm thinking of the days,
I won't forget a single day, believe me.
I bless the light,
I bless the light that shines on you, believe me.
And though you're gone,
You're with me every single day, believe me.
Days.
Ray Davies, The Kinks, 1968.

Edgar and Susan

An Excerpt from The Memoirs of Moses Pate

CHAPTER 1

ON A FRIDAY

At the time, I was working with my brother Richard on Dauphin Island, Alabama. It was a Friday afternoon, and we were clearing the land for some new apartment buildings. They would be called "condominiums." With an old D-6 Caterpillar bulldozer, I was pushing down a stand of enormous pine trees when I heard a large flock of crows screaming overhead. I remember being very amused at the way they were acting.

I was looking up at them when I noticed a big, dark, thick spot way up the tallest tree on the property; it was about two hundred feet away. As I pushed over each tree, the crow calls became louder and louder and became even frantic! It only then occurred to me that I was working closer and closer to a crow's nest. I had grown up in the country, so I knew that finding a crow's nest was a pretty rare thing, and judging by the way these big, black birds were acting, I knew that there must be some young chicks up there.

Just thinking of what I was about to do was odious to me. Because of the nest, I did not want to take that tree down, but I knew that nobody in charge of the job site would give a hoot about destroying the habitat of such magnificent animals. Conservation and ecology weren't big issues in those days.

After clearing the underbrush and willow trees, I approached the crow's nest tree with my dozer. It was then that I realized just how big this tree was. Its girth was amazing! I figured that it had to be hundreds of years old, and then I let my feelings get the best of me. I stopped the dozer, got down, and walked all the way over to the job superintendent's office trailer. I went inside.

This guy was an old, retired US army major who went out of his way to act as if he didn't like anybody. But like me or not, I knew that he valued my skill. So I told him about the old, virgin pine that should be left standing because it was a monument, and it might even enhance the property value. He just stared at me for a moment with a look of disdain that the "greatest generation" held for young folks who were products of the 1950s and '60s.

He then softened a little and unrolled the thick set of blueprints of the job. After studying it a bit, he pointed at the spot and said, "Look at this. That tree is right in the middle of where the tennis court will be." And without pausing, he added, "Take it down."

I said, "Does it matter that there's a crows' nest in the top of it?"

He looked at me with one eye half closed and said, "Look, I know what you're trying to get at, but it can't be helped. Take it down."

I knew that I had to do what I had to do.

Walking back across the property, I could see the crows sitting and cawing in the top of the tree. Perhaps they thought that they had been given a reprieve. I remember having a sick feeling down in my stomach.

I cranked the dozer back up and opened up the throttle. Then I started working my way around the tree, breaking the big, lateral roots with the corner of the blade. Like many old dozers, this one didn't have a safety cab, so I was able to look up and see the crows. Some of them were sitting in the tops of other trees, but many were still flying around the top of this tree.

After digging down to loosen the stump, I started mounding up a big pile of dirt in front of the tree in order to climb up with the dozer to get the blade as high as possible on the trunk of the tree for better leverage.

You're not going to just push a tree that big over, so after climbing up on the mound of dirt, instead of just banging into it, you set the blade and push, trying not to spin your tracks. You don't want to break traction. Then you stop, back up, and push again until it starts swaying. You time the pushes to get it swaying more and more until you hear and feel the roots under you start to crack. You repeat this over and over until the tree finally starts to fall.

Now this must have been the do-or-die signal for the crows, because when that root made a loud snap—and it was loud, because I heard it over the unmuffled, straight-pipe exhaust noise of the dozer—they began attacking.

The crows left the canopy of the trees and started diving down and flying around the dozer. There must have been a couple of dozen crows. Some would fly toward me in a dive with their claws extended in front, as if they were going to pounce. But just at the last moment, when they would be about ten to fifteen feet away, their wings would open up and catch air like a parachute brake. They would fold their wings back and zoom over, trying to intimidate me

Now I'm not afraid of birds, but it all happened so fast that the heebie-jeebies kicked in! This went on for a few seconds, and then they withdrew and flew away to the other side of the property. It seemed they had abandoned their tree.

I was about to gather myself to go back to work on the tree, when I turned around and saw Richard (who was operating the other dozer) running toward me. He had been clearing out a ditch about three to four hundred yards away and had seen the whole thing. When he made it to me, he asked, "What in the heck was that all about?"

I told him about the crows' nest, and we agreed that we had never seen crows—or for that matter, anything—act like that before. We looked all around in the tree but still couldn't see any young crows up there.

After a while Richard said, "I gotta get back to work."

"Yeah, me too," I said.

5

I got back on the dozer and soon had the tree violently swaying back and forth. Just before the final heave that would bring the tree crashing down, I leaned over and looked way up into the tiptop branches of the tree, and that was the first time I saw him. Because of the angle of the now leaning tree, I could see where I couldn't see before. Right out on those tiptop branches, just above the thick spot of the nest, I saw a large, shiny, black crow.

What happened next took only a few seconds, but it all seemed to be in slow motion. I saw the crow holding on for dear life. He had both wings awkwardly stretched out, as if he was trying to keep his balance. I yelled out, "Let go! Fly away! Why won't you just let go and fly away?"

The tree had gone past the point of no return. It seemed to be falling slowly, while the earth began to bulge up at its base. When the giant stump finally popped out of the ground, it was as if something had reached up and snatched the tree out of the air, pulling the branch right out of the crow's grip.

As the tree slammed into the ground, the crow clumsily flapped and fluttered in circles all the way to the ground. He jumped up and tried to hop and flap away. He quickly made his way into some underbrush and vines, and I could tell that he was trapped as he thrashed about. I realized that although he was a big bird, he was still a helpless juvenile and would not survive by himself.

I jumped off the dozer and ran over to untangled him from the vines and briars. The whole time, he was biting me on my hands. When I pulled him out, I put my hands down over his wings and body, trying not to injure him. That brought the other crows back, screaming and swooping around overhead. My crow looked up and gave out a long, loud *caw*. I remember thinking, *quoth the raven*, from the Edgar Allan Poe poem.

Right then and there, without knowing what I was doing, I had just met one of the best friends that I would ever have. Most of all, I certainly didn't realize that my previously noted prayer had just been answered.

I looked down at the bird in my hands and said, "I'm gonna call you Edgar."

CHAPTER 2

I GOTTA TAKE CARE OF THIS BIRD

I was down on my knees in the mud, holding a crow. He was still thrashing and jerking, trying his best to get away, and I couldn't blame him. He made squeaking and squealing noises that sounded like he was terrified.

I said to him, "It's all right, boy. You'll be okay." I think I was just trying to convince myself because all the while I was thinking, What in the world am I doing? What am I supposed to do now?

A feeling of overwhelming guilt came over me. I knew that young birds usually die when taken from their nests. I said out loud, "Let nature take its course." Hopefully, since this bird was so big, maybe his parents would be able to feed him on the ground. I was on the verge of letting him go when I looked up and saw something that pretty much settled everything for Edgar and me.

What occurred next I didn't understand then, and to this day, I still don't know what or why it happened. The crows that had been cawing, screaming, circling, and swooping around, flew up high, gathered together into a large flock, and flew away. No more cawing, no noise at all; they simply flew over the little back bay and disappeared toward the mainland to the north. I didn't know what to make of it. I can only imagine that they were heartbroken.

I held Edgar while I checked out the nest and looked around under the tree to see if there were any more young ones. There were none. Richard came back over to take a look at Edgar. He laughed and said, "Looks like trouble to me. What you gonna do now?"

I said, "I don't know. All I know is that I gotta take care of this bird."

Richard then said, "It don't make no sense. Only one nest and only one bird, and he had a whole flock looking after him. Must have been like crow royalty or something."

I replied, "I don't know nothing about crows."

That was the part that worried me. I knew that I had to take care of Edgar. I knew that crows were supposed to be very smart birds, but I didn't know anything about them! I started thinking about how in about eight months I was going to have a human baby, but in the meanwhile I had to raise a bird baby. I decided to put Edgar in the job site toolshed. He'd be warm in there while I finished out the day.

The shed was about a quarter mile away, so I was walking at a very brisk pace and Edgar was biting me on my arms. I had a long, red beard that just about reached to my waist, and he was biting and pulling on that too. I was talking to him and trying to calm him down a bit, and after only about a hundred yards or so, he stuck his head under my beard and I felt his little body start to relax. He became totally silent— almost limp. Now I was worried that he might have been internally injured during his fall and that he probably was about to die. I felt his body breathing all right, but I was becoming pretty bummed out about the whole thing.

He had been way up in his nest, being fed by his parents, soon to be able to soar above the world and look down with pity at us poor earthbound humans, and just being a crazy crow in general. Then along came this big yellow machine that knocked down his home, and he was scooped up by one of those human beasts. For all I know, he figured that I was probably going to eat him!

Right before I got to the shed, I picked up some straw, then went into the shed and made him a nest in the corner. I laid him in the nest and stroked him on the head with my finger. Suddenly, while I was still squatting down, he hopped on my leg, dug his claws into my leg, and stuck his head back under my beard. It happened so fast that it startled me a bit, but somehow—and thankfully—I didn't flinch.

I reached down and started petting him on the back. I said out loud (in the vernacular of the day), "Man, this is really far out!" It was about three o'clock, and I knew that I had to get back to my dozer. I also figured I was going to get chewed out for taking a break, no matter what I was doing—and I did. But I couldn't wait to knock off so I could see about my bird.

I always had on my mind my beautiful wife and my new baby coming, but now I was making room in my head about what I was going to do about this bird. This black crow in the toolshed had maneuvered himself into a little spot in my heart. While finishing out the workday, I had done a lot of pondering over the matter, and I decided that no matter what happened, I would not cage my bird. That would just not be right. I would do my best to keep him alive, and if he actually made it through and lived, as soon as he learned to fly I was going to let him have his freedom. I would let him go.

We did and still do live in the westernmost part of Mobile County, Alabama, a few miles north the small village of Tanner-Williams, down in a beautiful bottom called Peaceful Valley. There are great stands of huge pines interspersed with hardwood trees and thick undergrowth, sectioned off by three small creeks that come together into one down at the back corner of our land.

Peaceful Valley Creek

There were usually several big flocks of crows that had always made themselves kings of the canopy, so I hoped that Edgar would be all right and have plenty of company when I let him go. However, there was no guarantee of that. One year the treetops might be full of crows, but sometimes a year or two might go by without a single crow at all, and I hadn't recalled seeing any that spring—not yet, anyway.

We knocked off just before dusk. I walked my dozer over beside the shed where we parked them. When Richard arrived a few minutes later to park his dozer, I got down and told him, "I want to show you something." When I opened the door, Edgar was screaming and bouncing off the walls. I guess the sound of the dozers outside must have frightened him real bad. I caught him and held him close and started talking to him. He was biting and scratching, but when I put my beard over his head, he calmed down just like before.

Richard laughed and said, "Well, I'll be. He thinks your beard is a nest."

I put Edgar in an oil case box. Then we got in Richard's truck and made the hour-and-a-half ride home. Edgar had been totally silent all the way home. I would peek in the box every now and then to make sure he was okay. He seemed to be sound asleep. Birds go to sleep when the sun goes all the way down. Growing up on a farm, you learn the term "gone to roost." Well, I reckoned that Edgar had gone to roost and would probably just sleep on through the night. Well, I reckoned wrong.

CHAPTER 3

"WHAT HAVE YOU GOT IN THAT BOX?"

When Richard pulled into my yard, I picked up the box from the floorboard, then I got out and started up my little redbrick sidewalk. I felt Edgar trying to run inside the box. I heard his feet as they made scratching noises on the cardboard, and by the time I started up the steps to the door, he was bouncing and banging around against the box sides. I opened the door and walked in the kitchen, and there stood my little wife, Susan. She saw the box, and probably judging from the way the box was jostling around in my hands, she knew that I had something alive in there.

Instead of her normal, "Did you have a nice day?" she said, "What have you got in that box?" with just a hint of disgust in her eyes and voice. She had already had more than her fair share of me bringing home troublesome animals like raccoons, possums, moles, snakes, and so on.

"I got a bird, sweetheart. I got a crow baby!" I said as I put the box down on the counter. I was trying to sound enthusiastic and excited, sort of like I was trying to sell her something. Looking up at her, I could tell that she wasn't in a buying mood.

Now you have to understand, we're talking about the finest little girl that God ever made. She was always a lot of fun. It's not that she was being a crank or anything like that. Hard to explain, but it's sort of like since the very first day that she found out that she was "expecting," there was no more time for any nonsense. It seems funny to me now, but looking back she reminded me of Holly Hunter in the movie *Raising Arizona*, saying, "We got a family now." Of course, Susan wasn't innocent either. Here's a little example.

One Sunday night about a year before we were married, we left church early and had only gone a few miles down the road when a big possum—and I mean a *real big* possum—crossed the road in front of my car.

Without even thinking, I slammed on the brakes, stopped the car, and jumped out. I said to Susan, "Here, baby, slide over here behind the wheel; hold the headlights on him while I grab him." I could hear her laughing while I proceeded to catch the possum, using the proper possum-catching technique. I ran over and just before he disappeared into the tall grass, I swiftly grabbed him by his prehensile tail, while all in one motion I began to gently swing him around just fast enough so that the g-force kept his head from coming around and giving me a nasty bite. At that point I was yelling, "Open the trunk!"

Susan was laughing so hard and yet so beautifully that, oh man, it sounded like music to me. Anyway, she jumped out and opened the trunk as I tossed the possum in and slammed the trunk shut. Then we sat in the car, laughing our heads off! She called me crazy, and I said, "Oh yeah, well you're crazy too—you held the wheel; you opened the trunk!" Okay, there we were, sitting on the side of the road with a big possum in the trunk, and naturally this called for some kind of prank!

Now, I forgot to tell you that Susan was a little city girl. She grew up in a subdivision, lived a quarter mile from the local Baptist church, the whole routine. When we met, for me it was love at first sight, but for her it took a lot more looking. I sort of suspected that she was attracted to me—a wild, crazy, red-headed country boy—out of some kind of infatuation because I was different from the boys she had grown up and gone to school with. I learned that a little mischievous streak in her made her so much fun to be with.

Okay, back to the possum. This may have been her idea; I can't remember, but I think it was. We realized that it was Sunday night and church hadn't let out yet, so we headed out for the brand-new McDonald's just up from her neighborhood. We pulled in and parked by the back door. It was perfect. The place was empty. She went in the back door and took a seat right beside the bathroom. I was outside hovering over the trunk of the car, when she gave me the "all's clear" wave.

I quickly opened the trunk, grabbed the possum using the "technique," and ran through the back door and straight to the bathroom doors. I opened the women's door and slid the hissing animal right under a partition into a toilet stall. Then I walked out calmly, right past Susan, who was holding her hands over her mouth to keep from bursting out laughing, and up to the serving counter where I ordered two Cokes. No one had seen a thing. I walked back to our booth and sat down with Susan, waiting for the show to begin.

In those days, when Sunday night church let out, there would be a rush or stampede to the McDonald's on Moffat Road. It was the hangout for all of West Mobile. We were sitting in the back waiting for the rush. Then it started. The parking lot quickly filled with cars jockeying for the best parking spots, then everyone dashed to the doors to claim the best seats. After that, the girls started doing what girls do. They gather in little bunches and go to the bathroom together. Guys have never understood this, but that's what they do. So, the first bunch of girls went into the bathroom and immediately ran back out. They had trouble getting out because they got stuck in the doorway trying to all get out at once. The looks on their faces were priceless! It was a mixture of giggling and terror.

That's the way it went: laughing and giggling going in, and running over each other to get out. One girl hadn't even had time to … well, let's just say that she came out too soon! She was almost screaming as she said, "There's a monster in there!" This went on for a while, and Susan and I were about to blow up. We wanted to laugh so bad!

Then here came the restaurant manager. He went in, and then came right back out, except he was kind of white and blue in the face. He gathered up his nerve before grabbing a broom and reluctantly going back in. After about ten seconds, he was backing out the door. By this time there was quite a commotion breaking out in the whole place.

I got up and asked the manager, "Hey, dude, what's going on?"

He answered, "Th … th … there's a wild animal in the girls' bathroom!"

That was my cue. I said, "Stand aside, dude; let me handle this."

I went in and there was the possum, but this time he was backed up in the corner and really mad. "Be careful," the manager yelled.

I said, "Give me that broom." I turned the possum around, grabbed his tail, and using the possum "technique," emerged out of the bathroom. I quickly went out the back door and made my way to the patch of woods where the Dumpster was. That was where I let the possum go.

When I got back in the restaurant, the manager and everybody was treating me like a superhero. You would have thought that I had just wrestled a tiger! It was so cool. Susan could finally let it go, and she was about to die laughing. She had tears running down her pretty face, and the manager said that we could have a free Big Mac and Coke every Sunday night from now on.

Well, you know where we ate on Sunday nights. It was hilarious, but you know I began to think after a couple of months that the man knew that he had been had. It eventually fizzled out when they hired a new manager.

Anyway, I told you this story to let you know about Susan, so you could understand how Edgar would soon also fall under her spell.

CHAPTER 4

THE BREAKTHROUGH

Alright, here we go. I opened the box, and Edgar went insane. He jumped out of the box, hit the floor, and started thrashing around on the floor. It was kinda like when you drop a goldfish, except this goldfish jumped up on the counter and started knocking over lamps and the coffeepot and banging pots and pans. It was absolute mayhem! I couldn't do anything to calm him down. Every time I tried, he would bite and sink his claws right through the skin on my arms and hands.

I had said that I wouldn't cage this bird, but I was soon on the phone asking Richard if I could borrow their birdcage. He and his wife, Brenda, had a very large parakeet cage that they weren't using. Five minutes later, Richard showed up with the cage. We used wire cutters to make the opening large enough to get Edgar through. We threw a towel over the bird and actually wrestled him into the cage.

Richard was laughing and saying, "It ain't gonna work." Edgar was very upset. I think he was really scared about being in the house. I covered the cage with some towels, and he slowly began to calm back down. I remember spending a sleepless night, because I was truly concerned about the well-being of this bird. I couldn't just turn him out yet or he would surely die. I was determined to set him free *if*—and that was a big if—I would be able to keep him alive long enough.

It seemed like I had just dozed off, when around 7:00 a.m. I woke up to the sound of Susan's voice. I could hear her in the dining room, but I couldn't make out what she was saying. I got up, still a little groggy, and stumbled through the hall. There at the dining room table, I saw Susan with her hand in the cage gently stroking Edgar from the top of his head to the end of his tail. She was making baby talk … "Ooh, you're such a pretty bird … yes, you are." "You're so shiny and black, you're a good bird, you're a good boy," and so on. Edgar was standing up and he would rub his beak against her hand and his little eyes were halfway rolled into the back of his head. He looked so peaceful and he was making a little cooing noise.

I said, "Let me pet him." She pulled her hand out of the cage, and I slowly eased my hand in. Even though he let me pet him on the back, he acted as if he was tolerating it rather than liking it—but I still thought it was cool. When Susan started petting him again, it was like pure rapture for him. I mean he was actually getting off on it! Then Susan looked at me and said, "Don't you think he's hungry?"

I said, "He probably is. I wonder what he eats?"

It does me bad, but up till then I hadn't even thought of what I'd feed him. I thought for a minute and said, "I'll ride up to the store and get some worms and crickets." Back then, most grocery stores sold fish bait in the back.

Susan said, "That sounds gross; let me see what we've got." Looking through the cabinet, we were stymied until Susan said something about the scarecrow on the *Wizard of Oz*, and then I had one of those lightbulb-in-the head moments.

"Corn! Yeah, crows eat corn. We've got corn; we've got grits."

Susan was puzzled for a minute and then she said, "Oh yeah, that's right. I'll make him a bowl of grits."

She promptly started making breakfast, with an extra helping of grits. The kitchen soon filled with that wonderful aroma of cooking eggs, bacon, and grits. When she was done, I set down with my plate and Susan sat down beside Edgar's cage with a warm bowl of grits. It was a bit clumsy looking as Susan held a spoonful of grits up to Edgar's beak. She rubbed it against the side of his beak, but he wouldn't open his mouth. She kept offering but he wouldn't take it.

"I think I need some help." she said.

I reached in the cage and, holding his wings against his body, brought him out and prepared for what I thought would be a struggle. Susan rubbed his face with her finger and gently pried open his mouth and dropped in a little bit of grits. He held it in his mouth for a few seconds and then looked surprised as he gave an audible big gulp. That was all it took. He immediately started to *caw, caw, caw*, with his mouth wide open. He was acting exactly the same way that baby birds do when taking food from their mother. We had made our first breakthrough!

I sat him down on the table. He kept on begging and gulping while Susan did her best to keep up. It was like Susan couldn't drop the grits in fast enough. She would drop some in, then he'd gulp it down and again let out a *caw caw caw* with his mouth wide open. This went on and on at a frenzied pace for ten minutes. It was incredible how much this bird could eat! We were laughing and having fun while Edgar squatted and fluttered his wings. Then gradually his caws started sounding a bit muffled. That's when we saw that his entire throat was absolutely stuffed to the top.

Susan said, "Something's not right, I think I've fed him too much. I'm afraid he's going to choke!" He was actually overflowing with grits. Susan stroked his back and said, "Pretty bird, I'm sorry but I think you've had enough."

You really couldn't put another drop in his mouth, yet he was still making the cawing sound (except that now, the sound had something of a gurgle to it). After about another ten minutes of cawing and begging, he realized that Susan wasn't going to give him any more food, and he finally shut up.

Neither of us had any idea about the digestive system of a crow, but we could see that he was just about to burst. He looked like a small black bowling ball with feathers. Right then we were feeling rather proud of ourselves because at least we now knew that he would accept food from us and that his chance of survival looked better.

We were enjoying our breakfast while Edgar sat with his beak resting on his obese little belly. Then he let out a noise that sounded like *quaag, queeg, bloob,* and threw up his grits on the table. After that he looked up and started cawing with his mouth wide open, begging for food all over again.

Susan said, "You poor thing, maybe you're sick."

We didn't know what to do at first, but Susan, just to get him to stop making that racket, started dropping grits in his mouth again and this time she added little bits of hoop cheese, bacon, and scrambled eggs. We found that he would eat almost anything. He didn't particularly care for oatmeal though.

Edgar kept begging and eating until he was totally stuffed again. He threw up again and started screaming for more. Susan had him figured out now. She fed him about half as much and told him that would have to do. It worked. Oh, he still begged for more, but he soon stopped when he realized that she wasn't going to give him anymore. I think that he had made his first breakthrough.

I had been raised on a farm and had fed chickens, hogs, cows, goats, even catfish and geese, but I had never seen an animal gorge the way this crow could. At first, every time Susan got near him, he would beg for food, but she would only give him a little bit once an hour or so and he soon learned the routine. He even started taking food from me.

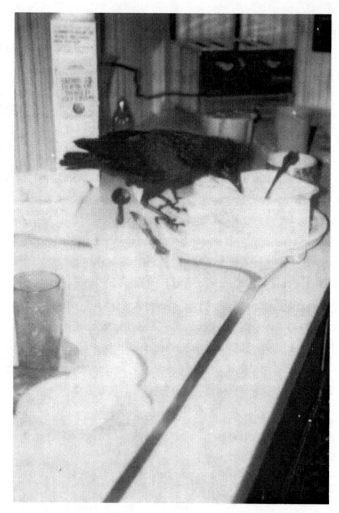

Young Edgar with his bowl of grits

CHAPTER 5

SMARTER THAN THE AVERAGE BIRD

About noon, Edgar started standing up and flapping his wings after his feedings. We had noticed that he really seemed to enjoy a piece of cheese with his grits. About three o'clock, I saw that during his wing flapping, he was actually lifting himself up about six inches to a foot off the table. I told Susan to watch, and sure enough, after being fed, he flapped and lifted up about a foot.

We talked it over and decided that we would sit on the sofa and taunt him with some food to see if we could induce him to fly. An hour later when he started begging, Susan brought some grits and set the bowl on the coffee table and pretended to eat some. Edgar started his begging, which to tell you the truth, was already starting to become annoying. He begged but we didn't get up. After a few minutes he was practically screaming, but we held our ground. He started flapping and bouncing and begging, but he stayed on the table.

Susan said, "Let's try something." She went to the kitchen and brought back a small piece of cheese. She started nibbling the cheese and just then Edgar lifted off the table and flew over and landed in Susan's lap. Needless to say, this was surprising and exciting, and we laughed at his clumsy landing. Susan started breaking off little pieces and feeding them to Edgar, but this time he was not making the begging sounds anymore. Susan was smiling, Edgar was eating silently, and I was just watching Susan and Edgar interact. It was all very cool. I felt completely happy.

I realized that I had found Edgar almost exactly twenty-four hours before he could fly properly. I took the cheese and placed Edgar on my arm. He ate right out of my hand. I really felt good. I mean, it was all very gratifying to know that I had saved this beautiful, magnificent bird. I also knew that I had an important promise to keep. There was plenty of daylight left. Sadly I had to take him outside and turn him loose. He could fly. I knew that he couldn't fly very well, but all he needed was a little practice and he would be able to fly away and take his rightful place in nature.

I admit that thoughts were flashing through my head like, *What if I could just keep him inside? Maybe he could be a house bird; perhaps he could be like a black parrot.*

I was letting myself get carried away, when Edgar finished his meal, stood up, and hopped up on my arm. He then stood up perfectly erect and kind of poked his chest out and simultaneously jumped and flapped, then flew across the room, landing back on the table. He looked so proud of himself. He would do a little strut, jump up, flap, and fly back to the sofa. Back and forth he went, from the table to the sofa, sometimes landing on my arm and sometimes landing on Susan's arm. This went on for some time. We enjoyed watching him as his flights became more proficient with each lap.

I was delighted with Susan's reaction. She could lure him to her with the sweet baby talk, and he seemed to go into a trance every time she stroked his back and chest. With all this fun we were having with him, I had already decided that I would postpone the promise of freedom for at least another day; however, I inadvertently did something that snapped me back to reality. I went over to the window and pulled open the curtains, revealing the cool, crisp, beautiful, sunlit spring afternoon.

I was right in the middle of some stupid discourse, like, "Very soon, my boy, you will be able to go outside and make some friends," and well, that's as far as I got when Edgar saw the outside through the window. Have you ever seen a little bird get trapped inside a room with a window? They go crazy trying to get out!

Well, Edgar didn't act any different. He was like, "To heck with this place, I gotta get out of here!" Problem was that this was no little bird. This guy was big enough to do some damage to himself, not to mention the dishes, Susan's knickknacks, and everything else that wasn't nailed down. He smashed himself into the window, thrashed around the room—and then he did it all over again! He had even torn the curtain off the window. There was just no turning back now.

Forget the cute little bird stuff. By now, Susan was yelling, "Get that thing out of my house ... *now!*"

He was hard to catch, and when I did manage to do that, he only wanted to bite me. Finally I got my hands around his wings and body to stop his flapping and headed out the back door. Edgar was screaming his head off. My first impulse was to just toss him down, but I hesitated. I started talking to him and saying, "Come on, boy, you're all right now. Come on, calm down."

He was still struggling when I remembered how I had calmed him down back on Dauphin Island. I held him to my stomach and covered him with my beard. I walked around with him, making little bouncing steps, and in a short time I could feel him start to relax again. Sure enough, while holding him and talking in a low voice, he started going limp. After about fifteen minutes, I took him out from under my beard. He looked at me, gave out a soft elongated *caw*, and then looked around at the sky and the trees. I became sad, and I think he knew it.

I said, "Okay, boy, we'd better not stretch this out; it's time for you to go." My mind was being flooded with the memories of the past twenty-four hours. I knew that in such a short time I had gained some memories that I would never forget; memories that I would be able to someday tell my new baby about.

Just then I braced myself with the fortitude of having a tooth pulled and tossed Edgar into the air. With each flap of those shiny black wings, he gained more altitude. This was just the kind of storybook ending that I had imagined. Edgar would fly high into the air, make it above the treetops, and slowly disappear somewhere into the deep woods canopy and find somewhere to roost.

But no! At about fifty feet up, he made a sudden right turn and fluttered back down and landed in the big oak tree in the backyard where I had a porch swing suspended from the lowest big limb. He just sat there midway up the tree, not making a sound and looking totally confused. I was confused too. Don't forget, in the short time I had spent with him, I had really developed an affection for him. I really wished he could stay, but I had already learned that I was not equipped to properly take care of him. I wanted him to live his own life.

I sat down on my swing to think. I thought of how young birds are often actually pushed out of the nest when they are reluctant to leave. It struck me ... *That's what I'll do. I've got to chase him away.* I yelled, "Go away, Edgar!" He just shuffled a bit. I got my fishing pole. I reached up and prodded him, but he just moved up to where I couldn't reach him anymore. You know how someone will pretend not to love somebody anymore so that they will leave for their own good? Well, that is what I was doing.

Unfortunately though, as with a lot of things, I have always had a tendency of getting carried away. That's when I had the bright idea of getting the garden hose. I aimed the nozzle at him and started squirting him with water. "Now go away, go on and get outta here!" Poor Edgar was getting soaked. He'd move around and I kept squirting and yelling. Edgar would climb up to the next limb and then the next until he was high enough that the water stream wouldn't reach him anymore.

Then I realized what a stupid and cruel thing I had just done. During this whole episode, Edgar hadn't even made a sound. He was way up high in the thick, leafy part of the tree, just looking down at me with a "Why me?" look. He looked so pitiful and I absolutely hated myself for doing such a stupid and mean thing. I was so consumed with remorse and regret that I could hardly bear it. I realized that Edgar was soaked so badly that he probably couldn't fly now, and to make it

24

worse, it was rapidly getting dark and turning cold. In a few minutes it was so dark that I couldn't even see the black little wet lump anymore.

Since that evening, I've done a lot of "what if" thinking in my life, but that night was particularly haunting. All I could think of was what a miserable death I had probably inflicted upon a helpless creature that I had so recently promised to save. It was unusually cold that night and I stepped outside several times and shivered, imagining what it would be like to drift off into a hypothermia-induced sleep and freeze to death. I didn't tell Susan what I had done. Oh man, I hated myself.

I got up early the next morning and went outside right after daylight. I closed the back door, stepped off the porch, and was heading for the backyard expecting the worst, when I was frozen in my tracks by loud *caw, caw, caw*s coming from behind me. As I spun around, I felt the chill bumps of joy climbing up my arms. Edgar was standing on the edge of the back porch roof. He was leaning over in sort of a half crouch, almost like he was aiming himself at me. He threw his head up and cawed at me as loudly as he could and then aimed himself at me again.

I was so thrilled to see him! I held out my left arm and said, "Hey, Edgar, come on down," and to my amazement he leaped off with only one flap of his wings and simply soared through the air and landed on my outstretched arm. I remember that as I stood there in the backyard, I took note of Edgar's weight on my arm, and I felt giddy about being able to interact so closely with a wild crow. What happened next is a memory that is so vivid that I can still clearly see it, smell it, and almost taste it.

Earlier I wrote that the night before I had not told Susan what I had done to Edgar. I had just sort of mentioned to her, "Well, he's gone." Susan had by now developed the most extraordinary ability to just let things drop. "Well, it's over and that is that." Even today, thirty-seven years later, she has turned that response into something of an art form. I have never been able to figure it out. Anyway, back to the story.

At that point, the back door opened and Susan stood in the doorway and said, "Pretty bird, you're still here!" Then she sat down on the top porch step. Edgar let out a soft cooing sound of delight that a baby reserves for only its mother. He lifted himself from my arm and landed next to her and then hopped up into her lap. Susan started with the baby talk again while petting and stroking him ever so gently. She looked at me and said, "Looks like we've got a little baby."

Up till then I hadn't allowed myself to think of him as a pet. I had done my job and had kept my promise to set him free as soon as he could fly, but now I was thinking, *This bird doesn't want to leave. He is still here because of Susan.* I stood there taking in this picture that presented itself to me.

There, sitting on the back porch steps, was this smiling angelic little lady. Her face and hair were partially lit by the early filtered sunlight as she looked down at Edgar. Her left hand held a small dainty coffee cup, while her right hand slowly yet almost unconsciously stroked him along the top of his body. Sometimes her hand would seem to just slip under him to gently rub his throat and breast. Edgar, shiny and black, was also being played upon by the slowly rising sun. He was sitting in Susan's lap with his head pointing straight up while resting on her stomach. His eyes were closed, while he made barely audible little *coos*.

I then realized, *This is not about me. This bird is totally and helplessly in love with my wife, and to tell the truth, I don't blame him.* I said out loud, "This is the coolest thing that I have ever seen … ever!" Then I told Susan," I can't believe he's still here." I told her about how I had tried to chase him away. When I reluctantly told her about getting him all wet and forcing him to spend the night that way, she just shrugged and said, "You're so silly. What do you think they do when it rains at night?"

I was standing there like a lump of clay when Susan scooped up Edgar and said, "C'mon pretty bird, let's get you some breakfast." She turned, walked through the door, leaving me standing there like a dummy thinking, *What just happened?*

This little episode was so profound to me, and I still smile when I think of the way that Edgar acted when he saw Susan. I think it reminded me of the way I felt for her. She was carrying my baby, we were about to open a door into a dark, unseen room and Edgar would shine a tiny, dim lantern into that room to give us a little peek of the things to come.

It had only been a few minutes when I heard Susan through the open door saying, "Don't do that" and "Get out of there," and then to me, "You'll have to take him back outside!"

Looking through the door I saw Edgar walking through the bowl of eggs she was going to scramble, and he had a piece of cheese in his mouth. I stuck out my arm and he hopped on while I picked up his bowl of grits and went back out on the porch. He looked like he had yellow socks on from stepping in the eggs. I was laughing, and I really think he was too.

I said, "Okay, buddy, I guess we've come to terms." Thinking about it now, my thinking that we had come to terms is laughable. Over the coming months, many times Edgar would prove to be an enigma. Every single time that I thought I had him figured out, he would compel me to do some more figuring.

I learned to be amazed at the amount of intelligence that could be wrapped up in a brain that was no bigger than a peanut. It eventually got to the place where I could always expect the unexpected. Sometimes I would have to stop right in the middle of something to realize that he would actually be playing mind games with me. At the risk of sounding like a dummy, sometimes I would realize that I had just been outsmarted by a bird! Susan and I would soon learn that Edgar was smarter than the average bird.

CHAPTER 6

A LITTLE ON THE FREAKY SIDE

Susan and I didn't go to church that morning, because she had a spell of the dreaded morning sickness. I had already decided that I would forgo my normal Sunday morning activities and spend the time with Edgar. You see, I was convinced that at any second he would just get up and fly away, and I wanted to spend as much time with him as he would allow. Normally I would spend my Sunday afternoons riding my dirt bike, but I decided not to "bust off" my scooter, because I was afraid that the loud noise would frighten Edgar.

Richard lived on the back side of the little swamp that separated our properties. He walked over through the trail that went over the creek and was very surprised to see Edgar sitting on my arm. At first Edgar flew back to the top of the house, but as we made our way over to the swing, he hopped along the edge of the roof and soon flew down and landed on the back of the swing. He would flap his wings to maintain his balance as we went back and forth on the swing. He soon learned the cadence and would lean forward and then back as Richard and I sat swinging and enjoying the company of this incredible bird. Pretty soon all three of us lapsed into what we used to call a lazy "Mayberry" mood. Every now and then Edgar would fly into the tree and then to the roof and then back to the swing. He seemed to remember Richard.

All in all, it was a lazy and enjoyable day. We did learn a couple of things about Edgar though. Susan called out the window, "Y'all want some coffee?"

"Sure," we said. I told Richard, "I'll bring you a cup." When I got up, Edgar jumped on my arm while I walked to the back door, but when I went inside, Edgar cawed and flew out. I said, "Come on in, buddy," but no matter how much I tried to coax him in, he would not come inside.

When Susan walked into the kitchen, he hopped off the porch handrail to the floor and walked—or rather, strutted—in the door, and right up to Susan's feet, bent over and rubbed his face on her feet, making the cooing noise again. Susan had a look on her face that seemed to be a combination of surprise, amusement, and annoyance.

"Okay, that's enough of that," I said because I was beginning to think that his behavior toward Susan was becoming a little on the freaky side.

That's when I made a connection in my mind. That was the first thing that I learned about Edgar that day. Edgar would not go into the house unless he saw Susan in there first. We experimented a few times, with the same results each time. He was afraid to go inside and would not go in until he saw Susan. During the testing of this theory, we learned something else about him.

Susan gave him a pet on the head with her left hand. Up till then she must've just petted him with her right hand or maybe somehow he just hadn't noticed her engagement ring on her left hand. I don't know, but either way, when he saw the shiny diamond on her ring, he went absolutely crazy! I had heard before that crows could not resist shiny objects. Maybe I saw it in a cartoon or something, but I did remember it from somewhere. Anyway, we found out the hard way that it's true.

He jumped on her arm and started pulling her diamond with his beak with everything he had! Of course, this caught us completely off guard. We had no idea what he was doing. I was trying to grab him, and Susan was doing her best to shake him off. I finally got him off her hand, but not before he had left little bloody holes on her hand from him gripping her with his claws. Susan was not at all amused!

This was the second lesson for that day, and this trait would later prove to be both painful and hilarious. Needless to say, Susan wasn't really very keen on the idea of Edgar coming back into the house. Another factor that I have neglected to mention was that Edgar had the nasty habit of leaving his little "droppings" just anywhere the urge struck him. Well, that was enough for Susan to start calling him, "Your bird."

Richard and I finally settled down in the swing to enjoy our coffee. I called up our little brother, Sammy, to come over and spend the rest of the day being lazy and watching Edgar as he would fly from the roof to the swing to the treetops, and back to the roof. As the afternoon progressed, he became more and more confident in his flight and also more comfortable with his new surroundings.

Late that afternoon it started to rain. I stayed outside for a while and watched Edgar fly to the top of the swing tree. I observed him settling down to roost in the rain, which made me feel all the more silly, just like Susan had said when she posed the question early that morning, "What do you think they do when it rains at night?"

I went inside and digested the day. All in all, it had been a very good day.

CHAPTER 7

OUR BIRD EATS LIKE A BUZZARD

The next morning, I woke up in much the same manner that I have for the past thirty-seven years: to the smell of fresh coffee and to Susan standing next to me with a cup of it in her hand, saying, "Time to get up." I sat up in bed and sipped my coffee while Susan prepared my breakfast and lunch. Yeah, I know what you're thinking, and I already know how lucky and blessed I am. I have always made it a point to get up early and try to give myself plenty of time to get myself ready for the day. Consequently, this has allowed Susan and me to have some of our best talks in the morning.

That morning we were talking about our new baby in her stomach, and about our new baby outside in the swing tree. We laughed as we recalled our strange weekend with Edgar. We were wondering if Edgar was still out there. For some reason, I doubted that he was.

When the time came for me to grab my lunch and go out to meet Richard, it was still a little dark outside, but as I stepped out on the porch, sure enough, I heard a loud *caw, caw, caw*! There he was on the roof of the porch. I could just make him out in the barely lit dawn. I held out my arm and he came right on down and landed. "He's still here," I called out to Susan.

She was smiling as she walked out the back door. She said (to Edgar), "I guess I'd better get you some breakfast, but you're gonna eat outside this time."

Just then I heard Richard toot his horn. "Bye, baby. See you this evening." I also said, "Bye, Edgar," but he ignored me as I trotted off to get in the truck. We started off on the long ride to Dauphin Island.

Richard asked if Edgar was still at my house, and then he told me that last night he had done some reading up about crows. He and his wife, Brenda, possessed what in those days was the fountain of knowledge. They had a set of encyclopedias, and they were only about two or three years old.

For you young folks, a set of encyclopedias was volumes of books that held just about all the knowledge of the day compiled in alphabetical order. A new set of volumes was printed each year in order to add any new information. Today, with something new coming along almost daily and being made available on personal computers, these old volumes probably seem quite archaic. At the time, encyclopedias under five years old were quite adequate. There were some computers around then, but they required two-ton trucks to haul them around.

Richard told me about crows being like cousins to ravens and that maybe Edgar might be one because he was so big. He also told me that crows ate something called carrion.

I said, "Carrion, hmm, I wonder what a carrion is? It's probably something like a mouse or maybe like a mole."

Richard offered his opinion. "I figure it's some kinda bug or grub, something like that."

"Well, whatever they are," I said, "I'd like to find Edgar some." I explained to Richard that Edgar seemed to be able to eat almost anything you'd give him, but he seemed to be particularly partial to cheese.

Richard said, "I'll ask around. Maybe we can find him one of those carrions." I asked if he had tried to look it up. "Yeah, but they weren't in the book," he said.

I said, "I've got a big dictionary at the house. I'll check it out this evening."

We arrived at the job site at about 6:45, but this morning the place looked desolate to me. During all the land clearing we had laid waste to the property. All the native animals—the raccoons, possums, and squirrels—had run away. I guess all that was left were the snakes and turtles that lived in the wet drainage ditch that ran from the road down into the little back bay. There were no more crows or any other birds to be seen or heard anywhere.

For the first time, I felt depressed about what we had done to the place in just a couple of weeks. The property had been so beautiful. There had been massive live oaks and majestic virgin pines, all seemingly laced together with huge two-inch diameter vines. Now it was a jumbled, wasted, muddy mess.

Still, we hadn't torn up the place with any sort of malicious intent. After all, a job is a job and we were only doing what we were being paid to do. This was a big job for Richard and me. We were subcontracting the job from another company, and there was still a lot of work to do, which was a good thing. Honestly speaking, since the last Friday afternoon when I had taken down the crows' nest, my heart was not in it anymore.

I now know that this had been an awakening to me as far as the destruction of animal habitats is concerned. Even to this day, I cringe when I see land being cleared. Down in Peaceful Valley, where I live, land has been cleared, swamps have been drained, and creeks have been dug out and dammed up just so that someone can have an unnatural lake or pond. My property remains as natural and pristine as it has for the past several hundred years or more. The wildlife, whether they are mammals, reptiles, amphibians, or insects, have their own ecosystem, and I just don't have the heart to take their homes away from them.

Okay, I'll get down off my soapbox now and get back to the story.

We worked all day and then headed home. I was anxious to get home before dark to see if Edgar was still there. Only about a half hour of daylight was left when I got out of the truck and started walking up my driveway. My little dirt driveway was about two hundred feet long, and after walking about halfway I stopped, set my lunch bucket down, and looked up in the treetops. I let out a loud, "Hey, hey, Edgar." There was no answer. I called out again, "Hey, Edgar," and there was still no answer.

I was very disappointed, but not at all surprised. I had known that he'd fly away, but I still hoped that he would choose to stay around for a while longer. I picked up my bucket and finished walking to the house. I made my way around to the back and sat down on the porch and started taking off my boots, while at the same time doing my last, "Hey, Edgar," call. I was thinking, *Oh well, it was fun while it lasted.*

I stood up just as the back door opened. Susan was standing in the doorway with a pretty smile, and she said, "You looking for this?" Now there was a pretty picture. Susan went over to the stove and was frying up some chicken. Edgar was standing in the corner on a sheet of newspaper, eating a bowl of grits. There were a few small cheese chunks on the counter beside Susan, and she would intermittently drop one piece in his bowl, explaining that she had to give them to him slowly so he wouldn't gobble his food so fast.

I just stood in the open doorway and took the whole thing in. I finally said, "How did you do this, I mean how did you get him to calm down so much?"

"Oh, he's just a sweet little baby," Susan said in her baby-talk language. Turning and bending over slightly, she said to Edgar, "You're a sweet boy aren't you, yes you are," Edgar looked up and cooed a bit while finishing his food. Susan placed a coffee cup filled with water in front of him, and he would dip his beak in the water and then hold his head up, allowing the water to drain down his throat.

It was very obvious that the two of them had spent a lot of time together that day getting acquainted. She told me that after her nap (after getting up early and making my breakfast and lunch, she would go back to bed and take a nap), she had gone outside and talked with him for a while. She said that sometimes he even seemed to talk back.

Then she told me how he would sit on her hand without gripping his claws into her.

Susan continued, "Of course, I would turn my ring around on my finger to keep him from seeing my shiny diamond." She had even gone to the grocery store, and when she got back he was waiting on the swing for her to return.

I said, "But I thought you weren't going to feed him inside anymore."

To which she replied, "I know, but he's been so sweet today that I guess I changed my mind." She told me that he'd been inside several times today, and that he would actually go in the kitchen to where she had the paper spread out and would poop on the paper. He hadn't pooped on the carpet or the furniture all day.

Now I was totally blown away! All this seemed crazy and just too unreal! I was tempted to pinch myself to make sure I wasn't dreaming. I was so incredibly pleased and happy, mostly to see how Susan was enjoying the whole experience. It was clear to see that Susan and Edgar were developing a very special relationship.

It was also obvious that this bird had an extraordinary degree of intelligence. I mean, everything about him was totally amazing, and just at that moment, I was thinking that it seemed inconceivable and perhaps even unnatural that he had figured out how to restrain himself and to relieve himself on the newspaper, apparently just to please Susan. It began to dawn on me that this was like living in an old Disney movie. I mean, who ever heard of house-training a bird?

I wanted to spend some time with Edgar myself, but it was getting dark outside. I held out my hand and he jumped on my arm. I took him out so that he could go to roost. He lifted off my arm with more ease than yesterday, and with one *caw*, he flew up into what was now "his place," and he settled down to roost.

As I walked back in, I saw Edgar's food bowl and remembered that I needed to get out the dictionary to see if I could find out what a carrion was. As I took the big book down from the shelf, I was still thinking about "carrion" being some small, fuzzy rodent or something. I sat down at the table and flipped through the pages until I found the word. I remember reading the short definition, and then with horror, slamming the book shut and just sitting there with eyes wide open with what must have looked like a dazed and confused look on my face.

Susan asked, "What's the matter?"

"Our bird eats like a buzzard," I said. I opened the book again to the word *crow*. It read, "Crow, carrion eater." I then turned to the word *carrion*, and read aloud, "Rotting dead flesh."

Susan just shrugged her shoulders and said, "Don't worry about that; we'll just feed him enough so he won't have to do that."

I told her about Richard and me trying to figure out what carrion was and what our theories had been. We started laughing so hard that soon we were both wiping tears out of our eyes. Well, it seemed pretty funny at the time. I guess you had to be there.

CHAPTER 8

POLLY WANT A CRACKER

I have kept diaries and journals nearly all my life. I jotted down events and things about Susan and Edgar every day, but sometimes I'm surprised at how vividly I can recall some of the smallest details of those days with Edgar. I think that I am most surprised at remembering the order in which the small events come to mind. There are many more events that I recall with the same clarity; however, it seems that the older I get, sometimes the chronology may get a bit fuzzy.

For the rest of the week with our new pet, my schedule was going to work after the good-byes to Susan and Edgar, and then getting home just before dark and saying hello to Susan and good night to Edgar. On Friday evening, Susan met me outside with some very small pieces of cheese in her hand. "What's this for?" I asked.

To which she replied, "Let me tell you what he did this morning."

Wait a minute—first things first.

Before leaving for work that morning, Susan asked me to open the windows that were next to the bed so that she could enjoy the cool spring morning air while she took her morning nap. There were no screens on the windows, and I opened the curtains about halfway to let in the breeze. She told me that around seven thirty she awoke to the sound of Edgar calling. She looked up to see him sitting on the window ledge. Sitting up, she saw a small piece of cheese on her blanket and then she found more hidden in the folds of her blanket.

She went on to tell me how she sleepily sat up and said, "Good morning, pretty boy," and how he then hopped through the curtains and with one flap of his wings landed on her knees. She was telling me about how she said to him, "Thanks for the little presents," and they had a little chat and how he was making the cooing noise.

Susan was telling me this and telling me that, but you know what? I don't think that I was hearing but just a few words of what she was saying. Looking back, I think I was having one of those transcendent moments. Please allow me to explain.

First of all, I was standing there looking at a girl who is so incredibly beautiful that it would make you throw rocks at a goddess. Secondly, how many girls do you know who would wake up in complete calmness to the sound of a wild animal sitting on their window ledge? We lived in the really deep woods, and most little city girls wouldn't have been there at all, much less peacefully sleeping with the window open.

Susan has never been easy to startle. Yeah, she would scream if you threw a rat snake in the bathtub with her, but other than something like that, she has always been one of those rare individuals who possesses the uncanny ability to take a situation; roll it around in her mind; assess the consequences and options; analyze a plan A, B, or C; then react in the most sensible yet gracious manner possible—and do it all in the blink of an eye. Then add the fact that she had a wild crow for a pet. Now all this put together was, you'll have to admit, enough to make one pause to ponder.

"Where's Edgar now?" I asked. She pointed up to his tree.

I called out, "Hey," It took a few seconds before he answered back with a single *caw*, but I still couldn't see him.

Then Susan called to him, "Now you come on down here and say good night to Daddy." (That was the very first time that she referred to me as Daddy.) Then we saw him move. He stood up, cawed again, and then slowly hopped his way out to the small limbs. He was pretty funny because he had his shoulders shrugged down and he was acting like a little kid when you wake 'em up and make 'em go brush their teeth before going to bed. He flew down and landed on my arm. I made some small talk with him while he was acting like, yeah, yeah, sure, sure, then he hopped over to Susan's arm.

She said to him, "Don't act that way to—"

I stopped her and said, "It's okay; let him go back to sleep." I was a little disappointed.

Susan said, "Aw, I'm sorry," as she tossed him up. He flew back to his tree and repeating the process in reverse, made his way back to his spot.

I awoke on Saturday morning to that pleasant sound of "Here's your coffee." I sat up to take the cup and started sipping. Normally Susan would go back to the kitchen to finish making breakfast, but instead she sat down next to me and started telling me about her plans for turning the spare bedroom into a nursery for our baby.

Now, some of you know what a spare bedroom can be. It was for us the place in our house where we put everything that we weren't using, but thought we might need someday. Today they call it hoarding. We didn't want to throw something away just yet, but most of the time, once something had been relegated to the spare bedroom, it usually became fodder for the yard sale.

So anyway, while Susan was talking, I was already making the blueprints in my head for the storage shed that I was going to have to build in the backyard to put our extra stuff in. With time, I learned to become quite proficient in the art of pretending to be interested while listening to such subjects as the proper shades of pink or the coordinations of the color blue, depending on the gender of the baby. Don't get me wrong. I was looking forward to fatherhood with a serious eagerness, but just at that particular time I started thinking about getting outside to see Edgar. It was no longer to see if he was still there. Now we knew that he was out there.

After eating, I scraped together the leftovers while Susan prepared Edgar's grits and cheese. I put everything in a bowl and Susan said, "Why don't you feed him this morning? You haven't had as much time with him this week as I have. I'm gonna go lay back down and take a nap."

As soon as I opened the door, Edgar landed on the porch rail. *"Caw, caw, caw!"* He was yelling at ninety to nothing, letting me know that I was late with his food. He jabbed his beak into the grits before I even had time to set his bowl down. He put his foot on the toast and started tearing chunks off. He would take a bite of something and kind of jerk his head forward, making the food ram into his throat.

Strangely, right in the middle of his feeding frenzy he seemed to pause long enough to delicately snip off a bit of cheese as if to savor and enjoy every little piece. In no time he had finished everything except one small dab of cheese about the size of a thimble. He picked it up and holding it in the front of his beak, he flew up into his tree. I watched as he made his way over to his roosting spot, set the cheese on the limb, looked from side to side for about a minute, and then made his way out and flew back to me.

"What's the deal with you and the cheese?" I asked. I mean, he acted as if cheese was like gold to him. You've probably noticed that this bird had something really strange going on about the cheese!

I walked over to the swing and sat down with him still on my arm. I started to put my arm down, thinking that he would just hop off. Instead he walked right up my arm and stood on my shoulder. This was the first time that he had been on my shoulder. I could barely feel his claws gripping through my shirt. I sat still, taking it all in, and soon I felt his grip relax. I began to gently swing and soon he sat down and became perfectly still. I admit, I felt really cool!

I remember thinking about a pirate with a parrot on his shoulder, and there I was with a big crow on my shoulder, which in my mind was infinitely cooler than a parrot. No matter, I still couldn't resist letting out a long drawn-out pirate type, "Arrrgg, Polly want a cracker!" Edgar had his head down and it seemed that he was also taking a nap. After about five minutes, Edgar stirred himself and stood up. He jumped off my shoulder and flew to a nearby limb and took a poop. He then flew back to my arm and walked back up to my shoulder. This, of course, blew me away!

"You are one fine animal! Instead of using the bathroom on me, you excuse yourself, fly to another tree, take care of business, and then return like the fine gentleman you are. Now that's what I call a true friend!" I was so impressed by the intelligence of this bird. I was going on and on. By this time I had lapsed into a rambling praise for Edgar when I noticed him leaning forward and looking at me. I thought nothing of it as I showered him with compliments. That's when I learned that Edgar truly had a very dangerous propensity for shiny objects.

You may recall the episode when Edgar tried to pull Susan's engagement ring from her finger. I didn't know what he was doing as he leaned over, intently looking at me while I talked, when suddenly, *zap*! He struck me in my "shiny" right eye! Luckily he hit me with a glancing blow. Reflex caused me to try to slap him off my shoulder with one hand while trying to protect my eye with my other hand. I felt his claws tighten into the skin of my shoulder as he tried to jab and thrust with the skill of a trained fencer.

I had no other recourse than to fight back. Grabbing him by the body, I felt my flesh tear as I ripped him off my shoulder. Edgar was flapping and cawing as I raised him above my head, fully intending to body-slam him onto the red patio bricks. Then, for some unknown reason, I checked myself and stopped. I let him go and he flew into the air.

It all happened so fast! I was up on my feet, heaving from pain, yelling and rubbing my eye. For a minute, I thought he had blinded my eye. Those of you who have been in a good fistfight know what it's like. The first sensation is like a blinding white light, which soon starts to darken as your vision slowly returns. That's what I had, and soon I was gradually blinking my vision back. In the meantime, Edgar was cawing nonstop as he circled overhead.

I sat back down but I was really mad. About then I heard, "Hey, man, you okay?" As it turned out, Richard had been making his way through the swamp and had just made it into the open when he saw me fighting with Edgar. He had broken into a run and arrived just as I was recovering. He didn't see the part when Edgar had "stuck" me in the eye. He had seen enough though, and said, "What in the world is going on?" I no sooner started telling him what had happened when Edgar flew down and landed on the back of the swing and acted as if nothing at all had happened. I even told him the part about the pirate with the parrot, and how I had let out an, "Arrrgg, Polly want a cracker."

Richard thought it was so funny and couldn't even talk because he was laughing so hard. As for myself, sitting there with a bloodshot eye, I wasn't as amused until Richard told me what it looked like to him, seeing me freaking out with a big black set of wings on my head. Then we had a long, uncontrollable laugh. One of those laughs when you don't have to say anything, and just when you think you're through laughing, you look at each other and bust out laughing all over again. I think Edgar was laughing too. Anyway, I know why you don't see pirates with crows on their shoulders—parrots are safer.

I had taken a camera with me that morning to get a picture of Edgar, but I had forgotten about it after the altercation with him. After a while Edgar went up to his roost and picked up the cheese he had stashed after breakfast. He flew out, made a few circular swoops, and disappeared over the end of the house in the direction of Susan's window. I ran to the back door and quietly crept toward the bedroom.

Slowly I opened the door and on the bed I observed Edgar breaking the cheese into tiny little pieces and then gently placing them in the folds of the blanket around Susan's legs and feet while she slept. I snapped a picture of him doing this. We still have it in a box somewhere. It was obvious that he was giving her a gift of what he considered to be his most valuable possession. He hopped back to the window ledge and called to her. She opened her eyes and turned over to reach out and pet him. This bird had what I considered to be an unnatural but genuine love for the beautiful girl. I went to the window, picked Edgar up, and then put him out and closed the window.

Susan said, "Thank you" and then, "What's wrong with your eye?"

"Nothing," I said. "I got caught in a saw briar."

CHAPTER 9

THE MOST TRIPPING THING I EVER SAW

I went back outside. Richard had started a fire in the fire pit. You didn't need a reason for a fire. It was just always good to have a fire going to sit around and poke. Pretty soon, little brother Sammy came over. Edgar had taken a liking to him. Sammy would come by after school let out to visit with Susan and to play with Edgar. He had been playing with Edgar every day that week, which was unusual because he was the only boy still at home and had the full weight of tending the farm on his shoulders alone. Edgar flew over and landed in Sammy's lap.

I said to Sammy, "See my eye? Don't let him get on your shoulder." I told him the story, and we all had another good laugh. It was about then that Edgar cawed loudly a few times as if he was saying, "Hey everybody, look at me." He jumped and flapped his way up in ever higher and higher circles until he must have been about three hundred feet above us.

I don't know if Edgar was trying to show off or enjoying what must be the glorious ability of flight, but he commenced to put on an air show of the flying skills he had learned. To say the least, it was astounding! He flew higher and higher in circles that became tighter and tighter, until he started flying what seemed to us straight up. He went up so high that he became like a black dot.

At that point he went into a stall exactly like an airplane. He then seemed to just fall. He rolled over and actually tumbled for a while until those beautiful black wings extended out and he began to soar down, picking up speed all the way. We ran out from under the trees and made our way out to the driveway, watching with amazement. He pulled out of the soar just in time to clear the treetops. I can't imagine how fast he was going as he leveled out above the trees. I don't know how fast a crow can go, but this young fellow was pouring it on. He started circling again, getting higher and higher, while my brothers and I were whooping and hollering him on.

I know Edgar must have heard us and was probably thrilled at the sight of us jumping and waving. Up, up he flew until he was even higher than the first time. Again he stalled out, tumbled, rolled, and caught air with his wings. This time he actually spiraled a few times before breaking into another high-speed dive. As he leveled off, he immediately went back up and soared around, treating us to an aerobatic performance the likes of which I never could never have imagined was possible for a crow—or for that matter, any bird!

The three of us were standing there mesmerized, letting out some of those deep-voiced "whoa's." Edgar was diving down again when he suddenly changed direction with almost a jerk. He maneuvered himself around until he was lined up with the driveway clearing. He came down so low that he flew under the limbs that hung over the driveway and headed straight for us, still going incredibly fast. He looked like a broadhead arrow point coming toward us.

I yelled, "Don't duck!," which was the prevailing urge, and when he was only ten feet away, he pulled up and went right over our heads. We actually felt his wind as he passed over!

He gracefully went up, circled around, slowed down, and came back down. I stretched out my arm, and he extended his wings out like a parachute and gently landed. As he stood on my arm, he had this proud look about him that seemed to say, "Okay, what do you think of me now?"

Needless to say, we were dumbfounded. I think each of us was struggling to come to grips with what we had just seen and experienced. In the vernacular of the day, Richard and I were saying, "Oh, man, how far out can you get; that's the most tripping thing I ever saw!" and so on. Some of my good friends came by that day and were introduced to Edgar. I always had friends dropping by, and we always had good times. Having Edgar around made the good times better.

I have always considered laughter to be like a kind of music. Even today when I hear my herd of grandchildren get together and break out in laughter, it is truly music to my ears. Back then, friends would come from all over, near and far to see the wild pet crow, and if laughter sounds like music, my little hill next to the swamp sounded like a philharmonic orchestra.

That day had gone by way too fast. By the time Edgar went to roost, about a dozen of my friends (not including wives, girlfriends, and kids) had met Edgar. As it finally got good and dark, Richard and my dear old friends Tony Smith and Buck McLeod and I were sitting around the fire. During the day, I had from time to time glanced over my shoulder to see an imaginary shed that needed building. I succeeded in putting it out of my head as we sat around stoking the fire and listening to Buck playing his guitar and singing old bluegrass songs till around midnight.

CHAPTER 10

ALWAYS UP TO SOMETHING

"Here's your coffee." I opened my eyes one at a time. Susan bent over, looking at me, and said, "Your eye is still red." I finally told her about being "poked" in the eye yesterday. I tried to laugh it off, but she didn't take it as funny at all.

She frowned and said, "Don't let him do that."

I responded with, "I didn't let him do anything; he just did it."

"Well, whatever," Susan said. "It's late. I've already fed Edgar; let's get ready for church."

When we left for church, Edgar was sitting on the back of the swing. The wind had the swing going, and he seemed to be enjoying the back-and-forth motion. When we got back, he was still on the back of the swing with a nonchalant look about him.

Susan said, "Looks like he's been there the whole time we've been gone."

When we stepped up on the back porch, we saw tiny pieces of aluminum foil scattered around. I told Susan, "I bet he's been up to something, and when he saw us coming back he probably dashed back to the swing and was just trying to look innocent."

"He's so funny," she said as she closed the door.

I called Edgar. He flew to me but landed on the porch rail instead of my arm. I petted him and said, "Hey, buddy, whatcha been doing?" He cawed real low and kinda shuffled around. He reminded me of Richard and me when we were kids and had done something to get in trouble but hadn't been found out yet.

With my axe and shovel, I started clearing out a place for the new storage shed. Even though I had picked a good spot that was straight out from the back door, I still had to chop down and grub up about ten or twelve small undergrowth trees to make it usable. I dug up the stumps and roots and started leveling out the ground, when Susan called me for lunch. When I finished my lunch, Susan put the leftovers, along with the scraps into a bowl for Edgar. I walked out and yelled, "Here's some food, boy." I sat the bowl down and went back to finish leveling out the shed area.

Normally, it didn't take Edgar long to show up when called to eat, but this time he didn't show up. I thought it odd but didn't pay much attention. It only took about a half hour more to level out the dirt. With that done, I was checking the oil in my scooter when I heard a strange noise. I couldn't make out what the sound was, but I could tell it was Edgar. It sounded almost like he was choking. I hurried around the house, following the sound.

Now, we had quite a few squirrels that lived in the oak trees throughout the yard. We had noticed that we hadn't seen any lately, but I just figured that Edgar had probably pestered them so much they had decided to move on down to the bottom where the undergrowth was too thick for Edgar.

When I walked into the front yard, I saw Edgar up in the fork of a limb of a big oak tree, standing on something next to a large squirrels' nest. I instantly knew what he was doing. He was standing with one foot on a dead, young squirrel. He was jabbing it and pulling off strips of flesh! The sound I'd been hearing was like a high-pitched gulp.

I didn't yell, but in a loud voice I said, "Doggone it, Edgar, we feed you more than you can eat and now you gotta go around killing my squirrels!"

I was mad at him, but I wasn't repulsed at all. I was surprised though. I remembered learning about crows being carrion eaters, but I didn't know that they were also predators. After some thought, I realized it was only natural, and sometimes nature can be cruel. I didn't tell Susan about it. I didn't think it would serve any good purpose. Edgar was indeed a puzzle with a missing piece, and for some reason, I couldn't get it off my mind.

There was another time Edgar would show his predatory instincts in a very unpleasant and gruesome manner. I don't like this story, but it is after all part of the story and I'm going to have to tell it just like it happened.

One day I had hemmed up and caught five very large green bullfrogs. They were huge frogs with long fat hind legs. I put them in a bucket and took them to the house. I figured I'd have a nice tasty meal with the ten fat frog legs. I set them down by the back porch and stepped inside to get a knife and tell Susan.

I would have been right in and out had I not been delayed. Susan and I had something of a disagreement. Do you remember how I told you that Susan was a transplant from the city and how she had adjusted so well to living in the country? Well, that only went so far. She let me know in no uncertain terms that she wasn't going to have anything to do with cooking or much less eating any creepy, slimy frog legs. I expounded the ancient argument of how they tasted like chicken—to no avail. She would have none of it!

Susan rarely put her foot down to anything, but once she did, you couldn't pry it up with a crowbar, and that's exactly what I told her. As soon as the word *crow* of "crowbar" came out of my mouth, I knew that I had left a bucket of unattended frogs outside too long. I hurried to the back door and opened it to a gruesome sight.

Being raised on a farm will usually cause you to become a bit jaded about killing animals for food. I've had to kill my share of chickens, hogs, cows, goats, or whatever, but I had been taught to always dispatch any animal as humanely and quickly as possible.

Now, I was standing there having pity and remorse for some frogs. Edgar had mutilated them … No, I ain't gonna do it. I'm not going to finish this. You can just use your imagination if you want to. That was one of the few times that I really got mad at Edgar. Well, so what. He didn't seem to care, and I could only blame myself because for Edgar it was only natural. Oh, by the way, I haven't eaten a frog leg since.

Okay, back to Sunday afternoon. I went back to "bust off" my scooter. I had been riding the motocross circuit for the past year. I have always enjoyed doing something that would induce an adrenaline rush, and at the time, these quick scooters did the job quite well. The season hadn't started yet, but I always tried to find time to ride on Sunday afternoons. I fired it off and let it warm up, but then I shut it off and went and sat on my swing.

Everybody needs a place to sit and think, and for me my old swing was that place. There were two problems I had to think over. First, the bike was a money hole. Second, the chance of injury was very real. These considerations hadn't deterred me at all till now. I was thinking about Susan and the baby. We simply could not afford for me to get hurt. We were making real good money now and had no debts except for a couple of thousand left on the mortgage, but I didn't have insurance and I knew that I needed to stash away as much money as possible. Oh just a little side note: I have been referring to our house rather loosely. We lived in a nice house trailer. We really loved it, but we planned to sell it after our baby was a few years old so that we could build our dream home. More about that later.

I got off track again. Back to the scooter. I really craved the rush of riding, but now domestic responsibilities were becoming an all-consuming concern.

I was deep in thought when Edgar flew down and landed beside me. He started preening his wing feathers, and as I watched him a thought came to me: *I wonder how old this bird is?* What I meant was, just like dogs have dog years, I wondered what a bird year is. What sort of life spans do crows have? I sat there thinking about how much he had learned and developed in such a short time. I tried to compare him to human kids and deduced that by now he must already be in his teenage years. This made me sad.

"You're growing up too fast," I said.

Oh boy, those five little words, "You're growing up too fast," would come back like a specter in my mind to haunt me while I watched my children and grandchildren growing up. I sat there motionless on the swing with Edgar. I looked at him, but he didn't look back. He seemed to be far away in thought.

I'm not telling you that crows have the ability to reflect on the past or wonder about the future, but I know for a fact that this bird was grasping the present. As I stared at him, he finally slowly turned his head toward me, blinked his eyes, and then turned away again.

At that very moment, like waking up in a start, I pictured my own child. Up to then I had a baby in a stomach. Now I began to think in a whole different manner. My mind went right on past the infant stage. I never saw a toddler. I wasn't imagining a male or a female. It's really unexplainable. It was more like a feeling than a thought. I think it was the burden of responsibility that was wrapping around me like a heavy, cold blanket.

Eternity begins at conception, and I was about to be the bearer of the terrible responsibility of guiding a living soul across the course of time that God gives us on what must be his favorite planet. It would take volumes to express the inexpressible. I had never had those kinds of thoughts before, and they were frightening to me.

Just then a familiar sound snapped me out of the trance. It was the *thump*, *thump*, *thump* of a Harley Davidson motorcycle, which meant that my good friend, Philip Brooks, was about to roll up. Philip was one of my biker friends. Today, a Harley is as common as a doorknob, but back then they were few and far between. The only people who rode them were bikers and cops. When Philip rolled up, Edgar took off. The sound of those loud pipes would make a hen quit laying for a week, so I wasn't at all surprised when Edgar flew away.

Philip was an old-school biker, tried and true. He wore enough leather to make a couple of saddles, and his dark brown hair hung down his back almost to his waist. This was before dudes started wearing their hair in ponytails. In those days, that just wasn't done, no way. He wore his colors with pride everywhere he went. He had all the paraphernalia of his club. He didn't have one of those ridiculous looking two-foot flashlights, but the faded place on the front pocket of his blue jeans always showed the outline of a .38 special.

Philip was one of those good-natured people who had a laugh so contagious that even Captain Ahab would have turned up a smile. "I heard you got a bird," he said as he swung his leg over his scooter.

"Yep, he'll be back in a little bit; you scared him off," I said.

Philip then said, "Somebody was telling me about you having a big black bird, so I decided I'd come out and see for myself. Hope I ain't disturbing nobody." He cut his eyes toward the house in a gesture of deference for Susan. He always told me how lucky I was for landing a first-rate classy girl like Susan.

I said, "Oh no, man, c'mon and sit down, she'll probably be out in a minute to say hey and get a hug." (Susan always liked Philip.)

We sat around reminiscing about school, talking about jobs, laughing about whose ole lady did what to who, when after about thirty minutes, Philip said, "Dadgummit, where's that bird?"

I really thought that Edgar wasn't about to come down as long as that big Harley was sitting in the driveway, but I said, "Okay, let me see if I can call him down." I walked out to a clear spot and yelled, "Hey, hey, hey, Edgar, come here." I held out my arm and sure enough, as if right on cue, he came streaking across the yard, pulled up, and landed on my arm. I was acting as if nothing unusual at all was going on as I walked toward Philip. Edgar had his wings spread out wide for balance. Philip had a totally surprised, jaw-dropping look on his face. After that, we had a full afternoon of enjoyment and laughter.

Edgar seemed to be enjoying himself royally. He knew he was putting on a show. Susan had joined us by now, and Edgar would coo up to her and would quiver and shake and spread out his tail feathers, which would send us into fits of laughter. He found himself in the mirror of Philip's scooter, and I think that he must have forgotten

51

that he was a crow. When he saw his reflection, he froze for a few seconds, and then he went into a rage! He started screaming and jabbing at the crow in the mirror. He spread out his wings to make himself look bigger. He was flapping wildly while slipping on the paint of the gas tank.

We laughed, but only for a moment. I didn't like what was happening. I jumped up, ripping off my shirt as I ran to the scooter. I threw my shirt over the mirror. Edgar was still very angry or very scared. The feathers on his neck were sticking straight out. I grabbed him up, held him close and put my beard over him. His breathing was labored, but he finally started to settle down. I stroked his back while Susan baby talked him.

"Well, I guess the party's over, man. I'm sorry about that," Philip said as he stood up.

"Not at all, it wasn't your fault; it was bound to happen," I said.

"Well, I hate it anyway," Philip said. "I'd better be going. Hang on to him while I crank up." He straddled his scooter and with a big heave, busted it off and gave a wave as he headed on down the driveway. As he made the turn onto the dirt road, you could hear his laugh over the sound of his loud pipes, which I thought was pretty cool.

About thirty minutes later, Richard walked up with a sheet of aluminum foil in his hand. "Uh oh," I said.

"That bird," he said, "tore the foil off my tomatoes." (He put aluminum foil around his tomatoes to keep the birds away.)

Susan beat me to it. "I'm so sorry," she said. Richard grinned and said, "This stuff keeps the birds away, but that ain't no normal bird. He didn't want the tomatoes; he just wanted the shiny foil."

I said, "I figured he was up to something; he's always up to something." I told Richard how he pretended to sit on the swing the whole time we were gone to church.

"Just like a little kid, ain't he?" Richard said. We all had another good laugh.

Susan sat out with me until Edgar went to roost. It was getting late. "Good night, pretty bird," she said as we started up the little redbrick sidewalk. She reached over and took my hand and laid her head on my shoulder as we walked. I felt good.

I could go on and on about people coming to our place to, as they put it, meet the man with the bird, but by now we knew that what they really meant was, to meet the bird with the man.

CHAPTER 11

DUDE, YOU GOT IT ALL

I used to think that flocks of crows were pretty much stationary. I thought that they were around somewhere just about all the time. I should have known better. A flock of crows might hang around all summer and then be gone the next summer.

When I first brought Edgar home, I naturally assumed that when I gave him his freedom, he would soon join the local resident flock and then he'd be gone. After letting him go, I realized that there were no crows around at all. I'm sure that's why he stayed around so long, but at the time it was a mystery to me. The crows were all gone, and they would not be back for what turned out to be a very long time. I thank God for that!

I believe that when Edgar saw himself in Philip's mirror, he had maybe forgotten about his family back on Dauphin Island. We were his family now, and perhaps he was defending himself from what he perceived to be a threat. After all, the crow in the mirror mimicked every move that he made, and maybe that's why he went to battle with this stranger looking back at him. I don't rightly know, but that's what I think.

One day I had decided to build a new septic tank in order to accommodate the place that Susan had picked out for our "permanent" house. That morning when I started, I had already bought the blocks and mortar. I would purchase the field lines, rocks, and pipe after another paycheck or two.

Early that morning, I started digging, being careful to throw the dirt as far away from the hole as possible, because by the time you get six feet deep, there's going to be a really big pile of dirt around the hole. It started out all right. I was digging with my shovel and chopping roots with my axe.

Edgar was alternately flying around and then hopping and walking around the slowly sinking hole. Down about three feet, Edgar figured that I was digging him his own personal hole to play in. He started getting in the way so often that I was becoming a bit aggravated with him. He'd hop in the hole and I had to be careful not to step on him. I was constantly saying, "Move, get out of the way," "Watch out," and "Be careful" and so on and so on!

Then he figured out that he couldn't get out. It was too deep to jump out anymore, and he couldn't fly out because crows can't take off and fly straight up. He banged off the dirt walls a few times, and then he turned into a crybaby, making the pitiful, "Oh, poor me" sound. I had to pick him up and set him out. Then I heard his, "Oh no, help me," sound! I had to crawl out of the hole and uncover him because a shovelful of dirt had landed on top of him. Then he decided to hop in the hole again. This went on for hours: putting him out of the hole, crawling out to uncover him. And the deeper the hole got, the harder it was to crawl out and then get back in the hole.

I had reckoned on digging the hole and laying the blocks all in one day. I could see that because of Edgar, this was not going to happen. To make matters worse, I was expecting somebody to show up to see "the man with the bird" at any time.

Susan came out a few times to bring me a glass of sweet tea, and she thought my struggle with Edgar was so funny. She would even pick on me saying, "You're sure getting dirty crawling up and down like that."

Eventually she pulled a chair up to the hole and started tending to Edgar for me. It took me all day just to dig a simple hole in the ground, and at about 4:30, not even having stopped for lunch, I was ready to knock off. At least I had finished the hole, but I was just too tired to start on the block laying.

Susan sat a glass of tea on the patio table and went back inside. I sat on the swing and tried to relax, but I was not in a good mood at all. Edgar was playing around, like what I considered to be the village idiot. He was acting silly and he seemed to be laughing at me while I was scowling and giving him the evil eye, when wouldn't you know it, I heard the sound of a car coming up.

I was thinking, *Please go on by; please be going over to Richard's house,* when sure enough, the car turned into my driveway. The car pulled up and I didn't recognize the car or who was in it. The car door opened and a tall fellow unfolded himself from it. I didn't recognize the guy until he opened his mouth. In the loudest voice possible, without yelling, he said, "Well I'll be doggone, well, well, well. I ain't seen you since high school."

It was Paul West. The reason I hadn't recognized him was that his looks had changed so dramatically, although his loud voice, laced with the most profane obscenities, gave him away in an instant.

I blinked my eyes a few times, trying to match the voice with the looks. In high school, this guy had been one of the neatest, most well-dressed, most immaculately groomed people in the whole school. He had driven a fine, new Oldsmobile Cutlass, always had a pretty girl on his arm, the whole nine yards. Paul talked loud and dirty, but he was neat; you had to give him that.

Now don't get me wrong. I wouldn't want to be one to "cast the first stone." I was certainly not what you could exactly call a conformist myself. I had long hair and a long beard, and pocket T-shirts, blue jeans, and work boots were basically my normal uniform. But there were freaks and then there were freaks.

Now I was looking at a "freak." He had a big giant shock of curly hair going in every direction, and holes in each pant leg and both knees. He was dirty, but not quite filthy, with kind of a sheen covering his face. Anyway, there's this extremely loud freak standing in my yard, swearing away at about a hundred decibels, saying, "I heard you got a big black bird. I been hearing all over the place that you got a wild crow. I been telling everybody, ain't no way. You can't tame no crow; crows are wild. Whatcha been doing? How you fooling all these people? I figured I'd come on out and get this story straightened out."

Okay, this guy was talking so fast and loud that I didn't have to look around for Edgar, because I already knew that he had split when this clip-on first opened his loud mouth. We called 'em "clip-ons" after the old clip-on neckties, because they kinda came along later. They had lived on momma and daddy's money for as long as they could get away with it, and when it finally came time to stand on their own two feet, they would just sort of wither up and try to follow the crowd. They always had a tendency to overcompensate because they felt like they had to do some catching up. "Clip-ons" were easy to spot.

Without even pausing to breathe, Paul said, "You ain't got no big black bird. Where's he at? I wanna see."

Remember, I wasn't in a good mood. I turned around and sat down on my swing. Paul followed me under the tree and sat down in a chair.

"Hey, Paul," I said. "Yeah, man, I got me a bird. A big black crow. Ever since you stepped out of that car, you've been running your mouth so loud and so fast, the fact is you probably ran him off. Now, I ain't seen you since we were in school, and if you think you're gonna come uninvited to my house and start running off at the mouth the way you used to … well, me and you just might wad up!"

Paul, clearly looking intimidated, said, "Aw, man, I'm sorry. I didn't mean nothing. Ain't no need to get ruffled; I just wanted to see that bird I been hearing about."

I said, "Stay right there, and let me see if I can call him down." I didn't even get up. I yelled, "Hey, hey, hey, Edgar." He didn't come down. I got up and walked out from under the trees, then held out my arm and yelled some more. Most of the time, he would have come down by now. "Hey, Edgar!"

Then I let out a long, "Heeeey, Edgar!" He still didn't come. I looked up in his tree and didn't see him. I looked around in the other trees and didn't see him anywhere. Paul was looking at me with this stupid I-told-you-so look going on. Again I called out, "Dadgummit, Edgar, where you at?" Still nothing.

I knew that Edgar was up there somewhere, and I also knew that Paul was the reason he wouldn't come down. So I went back and sat on my swing; I was bummed out and it showed. To Paul I said, "You scared my bird away." To Edgar, I mumbled, "Of all the times you pick not to come down, you gotta pick now."

Paul stuck a cigarette in his mouth and started trying to light it. Turned out that his lighter was just about out of fuel. He put it up and the lighter went *chik, chik, chik,* and each time the lighter went *chik,* little sparks flew out. You've seen it a hundred times as somebody tries to get that last vapor of butane out. Paul kept on trying to get the lighter to work, and I ain't kidding, it was really starting to get on my nerves! I was actually about to get up to try to find him some matches just to put a stop to that infernal chikking noise that was producing nothing but sparks. And this is the part when a bad story turns good.

Remember how Edgar couldn't resist shiny objects? Well, apparently sparks also qualify as shiny objects. It seems that while the chikking noise was starting to annoy me, it was apparently getting Edgar's attention. I can just imagine him looking down at the source of the noise and seeing those absolutely irresistible little shiny sparks. While anybody else would have given up and started to rub two sticks together, Paul kept after it until, unbelievably, the lighter gave its last bit of life, so I would have this story to tell.

Paul was sucking so hard on the cigarette that his cheeks were showing the outline of his teeth, when the tiny flame jumped across to light the cigarette. Who would have ever imagined that at that instant there would be an airborne crow zeroed in on those sparks?

Before the smoke ever hit the back of Paul's throat, what must have seemed like a big jet-black apparition flashed across his face, snatching the cigarette out of his mouth. I saw the whole thing. It was wonderful. There was no way that anyone could have dreamed up a more fitting introduction! Paul was screaming like a little girl. He sounded like he had been shot. He threw his arms up so violently that it caused him to tumble over backward in his chair, and yeah, he was still screaming. Meanwhile, Edgar pulled up and gracefully landed on the corner of the roof. And here's the best part!

Paul was now on his feet, slapping himself right in the face, not knowing what in the world had just happened! He looked up and saw what I was seeing. Up on the roof, it was a startling sight as Edgar turned to look at us. Somehow between the time that he had snatched the cigarette and when he landed on the roof, he had maneuvered the cigarette around to where it was sticking straight out of his mouth, and he looked for all the world like he was smoking it. He stood there all shiny, black, and proud with a little trail of smoke rising in the air. Even I was startled. It was absolutely the most perfect entrance, short of childbirth, that I have ever seen in my entire life!

Paul let out a whole string of obscenities, and he said them over and over and over. He caught his breath, and with his arms still waving wildly over his head, he started all over again. "I ain't never seen nothin' like that before!" If I had thought that Paul was loud before, I hadn't heard anything yet. He caught his breath again and then swore some more.

After a while, Edgar dropped the still-smoking cigarette to the ground. I calmly walked over and picked it up, and doing my dead level best to pretend like nothing unusual at all had just happened, walked over to Paul and calmly asked, "Want your cigarette back?"

Susan had come out to see what all the racket was about. So when Paul started up again, I introduced him to Susan and told him to watch his language around my wife. Susan pretended gratitude and turned to walk away. "Nice to meet you, ma'am," Paul said sheepishly.

She turned with a smile and said, "Thank you." It was obvious that Paul was visibly taken aback by the grace and beauty of Susan. By now he was totally subdued. He sat down and began talking in an almost soft voice. Susan had a way about her (that was unintentional) of disarming the most uncouth of people.

Paul looked at me and said, "Dude, you got it all." He didn't elaborate and I didn't want him to. He stayed for a while longer. At one point he held out the cigarette that he had worked so hard to light only to have it whisked away in such a startling manner and said, "I'm gonna keep this to remember today."

From that day on, Paul would prove to be a good friend that I am still proud to know. Edgar flew up to roost, and I explained that he always turned in early. "Okay," he said, "I guess I'm gonna be going now." I walked him to his car and we actually shook hands as he got in and slowly drove away.

I looked up at Edgar's place and said, "Good night, boy … and, oh yeah, thanks." I walked over to the hole that I had worked on all day and just smiled a bit. Then I went inside and had another glorious evening with Susan. Before supper I told her about what had happened outside with Paul. We laughed together till late that night.

CHAPTER 12

TAKING OUT THE MIDDLE MAN

I want to explain something about Susan's and my love and joy of being such a happy and contented couple of homebodies. We had spent almost two years together traveling from one construction site to another. We stayed in run-down apartments, old house trailers, and cheap motel rooms. I worked as a pile driver. Richard was the crane operator, and I was the crew foreman. Pile driver crews were one of the first crews in and one of the first crews out. We worked all over the southeast. We put in the foundations for everything from railroad bridges to shopping malls. Most of the jobs would last for only a month or so, and then it was pack up and move on to the next job.

Richard and I were subcontracting heavy equipment work now, and the job on Dauphin Island was as close to Mobile as we had ever been. What's more, there was a lot of work to be had in Mobile County at the time, and we felt so happy to be finally putting down some roots.

One day in the fall of 1974, I stopped by my dad's house. A man was there who owned a house trailer dealership over in Lucedale, Mississippi. I can't remember how the subject came up, but the next thing I knew the man was telling me that he could sell me a brand-new, fully furnished, big house trailer for only $4,000. He mentioned something about paying cash and taking the middle man out.

Even though I didn't have that kind of cash, I thought, *What will it hurt to talk to him? How can I go wrong by talking to him to just get some information?* I explained to him that it would take some time to save up some money. I even told him that I hadn't even established any credit. He was a curious type of fellow. He said, "Aw, don't worry about all that." This man told me that he would finance it himself (at an exorbitant interest rate, of course). I didn't want any part of that, so I started backing off. The guy was persistent if nothing else.

We rode over to my property in the woods. At the time there was only an old logging trail that ran through my property. I showed him where a good spot for a trailer might be. We wound up talking about hunting and fishing and stuff, but when we shook hands and parted, I really didn't give the matter much more thought. Oh sure, it was a good price—as a matter of fact, it was a steal! We hadn't formed any semblance of a deal, and besides, the thought of coming up with $4,000 was simply out of the question.

I went on home, which was a little old house trailer that we were renting from a friend of Susan's that she had gone to school with. I didn't even bother to tell Susan about the new trailer because it was just too far-fetched. I can truly say that the thought of the man's house trailer never again crossed my mind until …

One afternoon in the first part of January, I went by my dad's house and he said, "Have you seen your new house trailer?"

I thought he was making a joke or something, and I answered, "Nope, not a sign."

"Well get going over there and check it out," he said back. It still didn't register with me. Then I could see in his face that he wasn't joking. He was actually serious! I jumped in my old Dodge truck and sped off down the road. To tell the truth, I was thinking, *No this can't be*, as I saw where a big truck had left the dual-wheeled tire imprints where the logging trail met the road.

As I made my way down the small trail and turned onto my land, there it was. Somebody had backed a beautiful new house trailer right up on my land. There was a big cedar tree next to it where Susan and

I would sit and had even picnicked a few times, talking about "one of these days," types of stuff. I didn't even shut the truck off; I just jumped out and ran around the trailer.

I think I may have been slightly out of my mind. I ran around, darting back and forth and looking like a bird dog after a downed quail. Opening the door, I froze with a startled, gaping, open-mouth look. It had to be the supersupreme, deluxe quality model! I had never seen a trailer like this before. It was gorgeous! It wasn't happiness that had come over me. It was almost akin to terror!

I was saying aloud, "Where in the world am I going to get the money to pay for this?" I didn't dare step foot inside, because I thought I might mess up the carpet, and I thought I'd have to pay for messing up such a beautiful house. I stepped down and stared at it.

"Oh my Lord," I said, "what am I gonna tell Susan?" I was imagining how Susan would luxuriate in such a place. I started thinking how cruel it was for that man to do something like this to us. I kinda blanked out for a few minutes. I began to think of how I was going to punch the man out, while demanding him to get this house off my property before Susan found out!

There was a big brown envelope taped to the front door. I took it down and read the contents. It was the physical description. I thought, *What a shame and disappointment to be so close to something so nice for Susan, and yet so far away.* Then the lightbulb in my head snapped on. I told myself, "I'm gonna do anything in this world to get this for Susan. I will grovel to any banker who lets me in the door!"

I began to steel myself with determination. I won't bore you with the details because there were too many, but just let it be known that a Mr. Frank Pendergras, who was an officer of the First National Bank of Mobile, Alabama, patiently listened to my story and without any prior credit history, gave me the money to pay for the house trailer on January 17, 1975.

I guess I should stop here and get back to the story of Edgar, but since I've gone this far, I need to give you a quick preview of the unbelievably surprising rest of the house trailer story.

First of all, I had to set the trailer up myself. I had to buy and place the blocks that held it up, build the septic system, drill and put in the water pump, and hook up the electrical power line. Everything that needed to be done, I did it. We lived in it, enjoyed it thoroughly, raised Edgar while in it, and were quite prepared to raise a child in it, had it not been for a very unfortunate and unforeseen development.

When Susan had reached her eighth month of pregnancy, while I was away at work, a knock sounded on the front door. She opened the door and there stood two agents from the FBI. Yep, that's what I said, the Federal Bureau of Investigation!

Turns out that the middle man had indeed really been excluded. The man that we had bought the trailer from had simply backed up to a manufacturer's lot somewhere in Georgia, hooked up the trailer, and made a beeline straight for our property. The man went to prison all right, and they took our house trailer away from us. It caused us some unbelievable difficulties. I don't even like to think of it sometimes. I still paid back every cent to the bank, and paid it off early too.

More on this story later. Right now I need to get back to the story of Edgar.

CHAPTER 13

SLEEPY HOLLOW

Our time with Edgar was passing by way too fast. We had nothing but joy with him during his stay. Several months had passed and you could always count on him for a laugh, or at the very least, a smile. As he grew in stature and intelligence, my pride and love grew right along with him.

Susan spent a lot of time with him every day, and my little brother, Sammy, would come by after school and they played together like good friends. I always enjoyed when friends would come to visit. The circus part of strangers coming by had finally died down. I probably seemed rude when people I hardly knew came over just to gawk at Edgar. I got to the point where it didn't bother me in the least to tell someone that their welcome had been worn out and it was time to go. I did whatever I had to do for the good of my bird friend. I guess, in a way, it was just the same as any good parent would do.

I recall many days when we did nothing at all but play with Edgar. It was particularly fun when we played what we called "air games." Richard would stand at one end of the driveway and I would stand at the other end. Edgar would make his way high up in the air, and then he would fold his wings back and dive. He would come at one of us at a seemingly incredible speed. He would stay his course and make right for our faces. We would stand up with our arms folded to our chests.

As he got closer and closer, it seemed as though he was going to stab himself into our foreheads.

It took some nerve at first just to stand still, but at the last instant, he would pull up just enough to zoom over the top of our heads and we could feel a gust of wind as he passed over. Then continuing up in an arch, he would regain altitude, turn, and then zoom toward the other end, and whichever one of us that was standing at that end would experience the same thing.

It was exhilarating! Up and back again, we would do this for hours at a time. To stop, all we had to do was put an arm out and he would land on it. We watched him fly, soar, dive, and zoom around. It was almost like flying a kite, only a thousand times better. We played some other games we called "keep away." One of them went like this: We would take our wives' little makeup mirrors and reflect the sun at Edgar. He would fly at us in a frenzy. At the last moment, we would drop the mirrors into our shirt pockets and hold out an arm. He would land on our arms and start to frantically peck at our pockets. We would have him going back and forth as he desperately searched for the shiny objects.

Early into the first time we played this keep-away game with him, we discovered that he would get absolutely angry at his inability to find the source of the reflections. Edgar would jab at the hidden mirror and then he would caw and scream. He would get really mad. Not wanting to upset my bird friend, I went inside and cut up some pieces of his favorite food, which was of course, cheese. We resumed the game, but from then on we would reward him with a piece each time he made a lap from one of us to the other. This would turn out to be one of our favorite games, which Edgar also seemed to thoroughly enjoy.

Another game was played with glitter. Susan bought a bag of glitter that she was going to use for her nursery room decorations. As soon as I saw the little particles twinkle, I knew what I was going to do with them—they would be irresistible to Edgar. I stood outside in the sunlit yard and sprinkled out a small amount, which would bring him flying toward me like a black bullet. Just before he would get to me I would throw a handful into the air above my head. He would zoom right through the cloud of glitter, which created a shimmering vortex-like pattern right in front of my face. This game used to make everybody laugh and applaud.

One day while taking the shortcut through the swamp to Richard's house, I saw Edgar above me making short, hopping flights. He was trying to follow me but he couldn't make his way down through the underbrush and vines. When I got to Richard's, I told him how Edgar had struggled to get down to me on the way through the swamp. Richard came up with the good idea of chopping a tunnel through the undergrowth so that Edgar could follow us through.

So we did it. We chopped and hacked for two days. When we finished, Edgar could follow us all the way through. To stand on one side and watch him fly all the way through was a wonderful sight. In the evening just before dark, it even looked a bit spooky to see the big black bird flying through the dark tunnel. Richard dubbed the tunnel, "Sleepy Hollow." I thought it quite befitting.

One day as I entered the Sleepy Hollow tunnel, Edgar flew past me and was about to exit the other side when he pulled up and landed on the ground. I was watching him when he went into a snake dance. I had seen hawks and other birds like thrushes and mockingbirds do this before. He raised his wings high and spread them out as far as possible. He was hopping from side to side in a semicircle. Birds do this to confuse a snake by making themselves look as big as possible and to reduce the risk of being bitten in a vulnerable spot. Some birds will eat a snake if given a favorable opportunity, but some birds will only do this dance as a defensive maneuver when trying to protect their eggs or young. I just saw Edgar do it for apparently no other reason than he seemed to be picking a fight with something.

Now, I loved my bird, but I was just then thinking, *You idiot, you might be picking a fight with a cottonmouth moccasin or an eastern diamondback!* I ripped a long switch off a tree and started running. As I got closer, I saw that Edgar was in more danger than I thought. He was indeed a very intelligent bird, but sometimes his playful naïveté made me worry about him. In front of him was a very large alligator snapping turtle! Edgar was acting as if he'd found himself a new toy or something.

This turtle had a huge head with a giant parrot-shaped beak that was tucked in its shell. Its mouth was wide open, just waiting for Edgar to get close enough for a strike. He would have easily taken the bird's head off! I ran as fast as I could, and when I got to Edgar and the turtle, instead of hitting the turtle, I gave Edgar a sharp whack across his back. I hurt him and I meant to. He cawed and screamed as he flew away. After that I took a big stick and herded the turtle into the creek, where he promptly disappeared into the mud.

Edgar stayed mad at me all day. He would stay in limbs above me making weird squeaking noises, but he wouldn't come down to me. I really felt horrible for hitting him, but I had to do what I had to do. Every time Susan came outside, he would fly to her and sulk. While she would pet him, he would give me a little sideways look that seemed to say, "I don't need you." The only reason he didn't pout was that he did not have lips.

Later that evening, when it was time to roost, I was sitting in the swing, and my friend Buck was sitting on a chair next to the fire. Edgar landed on the back of the swing beside me. I tried to pet him, but he just moved away from me and then went up to his tree. I told Buck how I had probably saved his life that day. Buck laughed and said, "That crazy bird sure is good practice for y'all's new kid." You know what? Buck was more right than we ever knew at the time.

The next morning, while feeding Edgar, I knew that I had been forgiven. That morning Richard and I had decided to see if we could rake some crawfish out of the creek. It was pretty easy to do. We would rake to the bottom of the leaf matter in the creek and pull out the leaves that had fallen into the water during the winter. Then we'd spread out the wet leaves to reveal the crawfish and other small fish.

Almost all the crawfish were too small. There were only a few that we considered to be big enough to eat. We sat the big ones down away from the creek and flipped the small ones back into the water. Edgar was having a feast on the tiny bream and catfish that we were finding. We weren't having much luck, so we decided to put the big crawfish back in the creek too. When we would reach to get one, it would raise its claws up at us. You grab them behind the arms and they can't reach you to give you a pinch.

Edgar saw what we were doing and he decided that he was going to get himself a crawfish. I didn't allow Edgar to learn a lesson the day before because it was too dangerous for him, but today I figured that I'd let him go ahead and learn something. He started poking at a five-inch crawfish with his toes. The crawfish raised itself up and held out its open claws. After two or three pokes, the crawfish latched down on one of Edgar's toes. If you've ever been pinched by a crawfish, you know what it's like. The harder you try to pull it off, the harder it will pinch—and it hurts.

You would have thought that Edgar had been caught in a bear trap! He let out a painful yell and started going nuts! He shook his leg and then took off flying with the crawfish still hanging on. He banged into the undergrowth and was tumbling and flapping at the same time. When he finally got untangled and made it into the clear, he was screaming louder and louder. By now I was upset. I had wanted him to learn a lesson, but I couldn't bear to see him hurting. He flew out of the tunnel, turned around, and flew right back in. I was already running toward him yelling, "Edgar, Edgar!"

Just then he flew into me without bothering to land. When Edgar slammed into my chest, I got my hands around him and held him tight while Richard pried the crawfish's pinchers open. You could tell that Edgar's relief was instantaneous. He relaxed and went limp in my hands, just like when he had been a "little" crow. Once again I put him under my beard and stroked his back. Richard and I stood silent for a while. I became a bit sad, reflecting on the days when my "boy" was just a little guy.

He stayed on my arm for the rest of the day. I know that Edgar did learn a good lesson that day, because he never landed on the ground in the tunnel again. He had learned that there were animals down there that would hurt him. It was good for me—one less thing for me to worry about.

The springtime had passed on by and it was midsummer. Richard decided to have a Fourth of July "throw down." (That's a big party.) During the day, I had helped him build a bandstand, string lights, and set out washtubs for drinks and refreshments. Early that evening, people started showing up. Soon the place was coming alive. The band was tuning up, bikes were rumbling in, and freaks were gathering in their circles. Susan and Edgar stayed home. Susan needed her rest, and Edgar didn't like crowds anyway.

I went back through the tunnel to check on Susan. I was going to skip the party, until the phone rang. It was Buck on the other end. "C'mon over," he said. "I'm over here at Richard's."

Buck McLeod was my oldest friend. We had been friends since way back in elementary school, and we called each other "Brotherman." I hung up the phone and told Susan, "I'll be back in a little while. I'm going to see Buck." I walked back through the tunnel. Edgar stayed with Susan. When I came up the hill, Buck met me halfway. We hugged each other like always. I don't ever recall just shaking hands with Buck.

"Call Edgar over," he said. "Everybody wants to see him."

I said, "Aw, man, I don't know about that. He don't like crowds."

"C'mon, man, just for a little while," he said. I studied Buck for a second and said, "All right, I'll call him, but he might not come … let's see."

I walked up the hill a little farther so my voice would carry better, and I let out my "Hey, Edgar, come here" call. Then once again, a bit louder, "Hey, hey, Edgar." By now the whole crowd had hushed and was watching. I didn't think he would come, but if he did, I figured that he'd be coming over the treetops of the swamp. He chose to make a more dramatic appearance.

Caw, caw, caw. I knew he was coming through the Sleepy Hollow tunnel. Everybody was watching as he emerged from the dark hole in the swamp. As he cleared the low-hanging tree limbs, he lifted up high and then glided down and landed on my arm. I said to him softly, "What a ham."

When I turned around and faced the crowd of people—and this was a pretty rowdy bunch—they were all perfectly silent. Then you could hear random "whoa's" and "far outs." Then everybody wanted to see the crow up close. Folks started trying to crowd around us, but Edgar would have none of that. He lifted off my arm and landed on a high limb. Some idiot threw a piece of ice at him, and Richard promptly stormed over and started violently punching out the biker who had thrown it. He turned around, heaving, and said, "Don't mess with the bird!" Everybody started putting down the bleeding biker as he got up. He had the good judgment to get on his scooter and leave.

Everything settled back down, and I was ready to go. I called out to Edgar, "Hey, let's go." I held out my arm and Edgar flew off the limb, but before he flew to me, he landed above Richard's swing, where Joe Plate was sitting without a shirt on. Joe grinned as he looked up. That's when Edgar, I guess just to make his own statement, squatted and relieved himself right on Joe's belly. The whole place erupted in hysterical laughter.

Edgar flew to my arm and I walked down the hill and through the tunnel with him. He stayed on my arm all the way home. I took him to his tree and said, "Edgar, you're far too cool." He flew up to roost just as Buck walked up. As the noise of the "throw down" waxed and waned, Buck and I sat out by the fire and listened to bluegrass music on the Mississippi Public Radio channel till late into the night.

CHAPTER 14

THE EARRING THAT CHANGED EVERYTHING

I used to wonder what Edgar was seeing as he soared around high up in the air above our land. It was only about a year ago from this writing that my son, Daniel, showed me a view of our property on the Goggle Earth program. When I saw it, I thought of Edgar and said, "So that's what he was seeing; how cool that must have been."

That summer was passing on by. It hadn't been one of those "lazy" summers. Edgar had seen to that. I had finished the septic tank and hauled the pile of dirt away. Then I built the storage shed (even though Edgar had flown away with my level) and moved everything out of the spare bedroom into it. I greatly expanded the yard by clearing away the underbrush so that our soon-coming child would have safe places to play. With particular delight I watched Susan's slowly expanding belly. I had even taught Edgar to sit on my shoulder without having to worry about losing an eye. We thought that we had pretty much figured Edgar out. He would soon make us think yet again. We knew that he had figured *us* out.

One night, when Susan and I had finished watching our cloudy black-and-white TV, we realized that we hadn't been anywhere at all on the weekends except to church and Evans grocery and hardware store since way back in March when we had adopted Edgar. We had no regrets. We were so happy and in love, and that was all that really mattered.

Then a Sunday afternoon came along that would slowly, almost imperceptibly start a small series of events that would change things forever. When you think you've got everything figured out and all is right with the world, brace yourself, because nothing lasts forever.

I hadn't ridden my scooter but a time or two the whole time that Edgar had been with us. It was something about the sound of the big single cylinder two-stroke engine that nearly scared him out of his feathers. He would flap and his neck feathers would stick out and he would scream at the top of his little lungs.

Now, if I had been a cruel fellow I might have thought it funny. But I loved my living, breathing, warm bird, infinitely more than some loud, hard, cold machine. So I pickled it. I drained the gasoline out of the tank and carburetor and taped up all the holes to keep the dirt dauber wasps out. Not too long before, someone had come up with a new miracle product called WD-40, which could be poured into the spark plug hole to preserve the engine (indefinitely, I reckon).

One thing that I hadn't told you about was that Susan had a scooter too. She had a D-T125 Yamaha. It was an on- and off-road bike. I took all the lights off to keep them from getting broken. She used to have a blast, riding through the woods and down the old logging roads. We had a lot of fun riding together, but ever since the day she found out that she was expecting, she would no longer ride it. I tried to get her to ride, but she simply would not do it.

It was a fine little bike in excellent shape, and I kept it running like a top. It was too small for me to ride, so I decided to sell it. I put the lights back on it and placed an advertisement in the Sunday edition of the *Mobile Press Register* newspaper. I got up early that morning and had done some chores outside before getting ready for church. We left church a little early because I wanted to hang out around the phone in case somebody called about the little scooter.

By the time the afternoon came, I had only gotten two inquiries and I could tell that they weren't really interested. Around one thirty I got a call from a fellow that sounded real good. I described it to him, and he said it sounded like just what he was looking for. He told me that he lived over in Kushla and I gave him the directions to my house. "I'll come right on over," he said.

I figured it would take him about an hour, so I just hung around in my easy chair that was next to the front window. Every now and then I would catch a glimpse of Richard checking his fish traps down in the bottom by the creek. I was really feeling good. I thought to myself, *This is a real good day.*

Sure enough, in about an hour, I saw a car pull into the driveway. It was one of those huge old Oldsmobiles—a giant four-door car with a dump truck motor that would seem like a tank today.

I was looking through the curtain when a very tall, lanky fellow opened the door and got out. Now, this dude was really tall. He reminded me of Abraham Lincoln. I was gonna wait and let him knock on the door. (You don't want to seem anxious when you're trying to sell something.) Anyway, I was just sitting there watching when the door swung open on the other side of the car. I could tell that it was a woman getting out.

Now, I don't want to sound rude, because I'm not. I'm just telling you what I saw. A very, shall we say, large woman got out of the car and started to laboriously make her way around to the front of the car, and on over until she stopped at the front fender. This was a *very large* woman. She wasn't really short, but I'm telling you, she just about covered up the whole front fender of that big Oldsmobile.

This woman had a hairdo that was stacked up about two feet tall. That was, I guess what you call a style that was going on in those days. I suppose you may have seen Marge Simpson on TV. Well, let me tell you, that's really not too much of an exaggeration. Back in those days, some women would stack their hair up so high that it must have taken a whole can of hairspray just to keep it up, and I ain't kidding either! Heck, my oldest brother, Russell, had a wife whose hair seemed to defy the law of gravity!

Anyway, I was sitting in my chair watching this couple. The tall man politely waited for his wife to catch up, but I reckon that his legs were so long that he kept outrunning her. It was just as they were about to step onto my little redbrick sidewalk, when I saw the bright sunlight sparkle off a set of long, dangling, shiny earrings that the woman was wearing. I instantly thought, *Oh, no!* because I knew what was about to happen. I jumped up and ran across the room. When I reached the door, I threw it open, kicked the screen door back, and yelled, "St—" I was gonna yell *"Stop,"* but I never got the whole word out. It was too late.

Before I even opened the door, Edgar was streaking through the air. He slammed into the side of the woman's head. His beak was clamped down on the woman's left earlobe, and he had a death grip with his feet on that big wad of hair. The large lady had no idea what was happening. She had a startled look on her face that I can't begin to describe. Naturally she took off running, screaming like a banshee! It was, well, it was mayhem.

The lady ran down the hill a few steps and then she turned around and made a few laps around the car. She was beating and banging at Edgar. They were locked in a vicious, no-quarter battle. She still didn't know what was on her head, and the pitch of her scream was getting higher and higher! Edgar was screaming too, and he was flapping and jerking on her ear. She made another lap or two around the car and then she took off down the driveway, picking up speed all the way!

All this happened so fast that the tall man just froze. By the time he came to and made for his car, the woman had made the corner and was headed down the dirt road. The man gave me a quick dumbfounded glance as the big Oldsmobile cut a doughnut in my yard. The whole time that he was tearing down my driveway, I could hear two screams. One was the woman's and the other was Edgar's.

I went running around to the backyard, and I stopped long enough to get my bearing from the sounds. I had every intention in the world to go running to try and help get Edgar off that woman's head, but as I listened, I could tell by the sound that the woman had made it all the way to the highway by her now-distant screaming. But I couldn't hear Edgar anymore.

I heard a car door slam shut, and then the sound of the Oldsmobile as it accelerated up the hill. I stood there for a minute, and then yelled for Edgar as loud as I could. "Heeey, Edgaaar!" Richard had come running when he heard the scream and he saw the car roaring away. He didn't know what had happened, but he saw the woman running with Edgar on her head. He was laughing so hard that he couldn't catch his breath.

Now the back door opened and Susan walked out. She said, "What's happening? Who was doing all that screaming?"

Now I know it does me bad, it does me real bad, but when I started telling her what had just happened, I started laughing too. Richard and I were laughing so hard that we had to sit down on the ground. I laughed so hard that it hurt. I was wiping tears away and trying to catch my breath, and Richard was beating his fist on the ground.

Susan spun around on her heel to go back inside. She stopped and said, "Y'all should be ashamed." It was hard to surprise her anymore, but I did hear her laugh before she closed the door.

We laughed some more and then I stopped suddenly when a thought flashed in my head. *I bet my bird is dead!* It was sobering. I got up and yelled for Edgar again. I strained my ear, hoping to hear him *caw*. I asked Richard, "You hear him?" "Nope," he said. We jumped in my truck and headed for the highway. We got out and looked all around. I could see where the big Oldsmobile had left some rubber as it left the dirt road and hit the asphalt. I looked up in the tall pines that lined the road. I didn't see him anywhere and I called again … nothing. We went back home and I sat down hard on the swing.

Richard said, "I gotta go, but don't worry, he'll be all right … I hope." As he walked down the hill, he was still laughing his head off.

I didn't think it was funny anymore. I was worried, worried bad. A dark, bad feeling came down all over me. I vividly remember thinking, *Man, I hope he ain't dead.* I even started talking to myself, "I hope she didn't kill him. I probably would have killed him myself if something like that happened to me. … It was good while it lasted." That thought was unbearable! Memories started blasting in my brain! I remember holding my head in my hands, trying to stop the memories. I was more than sad; I was heartbroken. I felt absolutely horrible.

During this time, I began to take measure of what had happened. The thoughts of poor Edgar and poor me soon gave way to the poor woman. That had to be incredibly frightening for her. I tried to put myself in her place. If that had happened to Susan, I would have been out for blood! I thought, *She could have had a heart attack, or at least she could have collapsed from exhaustion.* My heart truly went out to her. I know you're going to think I'm a bad person (please don't), but I almost chuckled when I thought, *I bet she didn't know that she could run that far that fast.* It was about a quarter mile to the highway and she had to have set a new world record for her weight class.

By then I had been sitting there for more than an hour. I almost got up a couple of times to go talk to Susan, but I wasn't able. I'm not ashamed to tell you that I cried. I was doing "what if this, and what if that." I was being swallowed with grief and regret, and then I heard a *caw*! I sprang out of the swing and as I looked up, he was already descending toward me. I held out my arm, and as soon as he landed, I pulled him into an embrace. I don't remember what I said; I don't know if I said anything. I was so happy and relieved, words just can't describe what I was feeling.

Edgar yanked on my beard, which told me that he was glad to see me too. I thought he might be hurt, so I sat him down on the patio table and examined him as I stroked his back. He looked bruised and battered, but unbowed. He was all right. I leaned back to look at him, but he jumped, flapped, and flew away over the treetops that bordered our property.

This was the beginning of that series of events that I mentioned at the start of this chapter; it would change things forever. You see, up to this time, Edgar had never left our property. He had 150 acres to play and explore. There was my place, and Richard's place, and my dad had another piece of property that bordered us where Richard and I kept our gardens, but we pretty much considered it as a whole.

Edgar had plenty of room and variety. There were pines and oaks. There was a swamp, edged with hills and flats. I never could figure out how he knew where the property lines were laid, but somehow he knew. He'd see a squirrel running across the ground and he would pester that squirrel something awful, but if the squirrel made it over to the McGowins' land, he'd sit on a limb and yell like an idiot, but he wouldn't cross the line. Sure there was a fence there, but who would ever think that a crow would know what a fence was for. Even during the "air games," he wouldn't cross the line.

Richard and I pondered this many times. We had grown up on a farm and had just about every kind of pet that you could name, domestic and wild, but we had never seen any animal that even came close to having the intelligence possessed by this crow.

Okay, like I said, I had just sat there and watched him fly over the trees that bordered our property, and I knew what I was seeing. I knew that I was watching a page being turned. I stood up and took a few steps in the direction that he had flown, and I said, "What in the world, Edgar. You left the land—where are you going?" I was standing there doing the hands out, palms up, what's going on sign, when I heard him coming back, cawing all the way—but the caws were kind of muffled.

He came into view from the same direction that he had left. He came over the trees, leveled out, and glided under the limbs to land back on the patio table. Before he landed, I could see that he had something in his mouth. He leaned over and dropped the big, shiny, dangly earring! I nearly fell over backward. He was standing up tall, doing his proud what-do-you-think-of-me-now look.

I said, "You rascal." I reached down to pick it up, and he pecked me hard on the back of my hand. It didn't hurt, but I drew back anyway. "I guess you earned it," I said.

It wasn't long before he flew up to roost. He took the earring with him. I sat out for a long time after dark. Susan called me several times for supper. "In a little while," I kept saying.

I used to wonder how long Edgar would stay. I had started to think that he would always be around, but now I wasn't so sure. I felt that I had better start to mentally prepare myself for that day. Little did I know how soon that day would come.

One more thing. Over the years, I have often wondered about a tale going around somewhere in Kushla, about Big Grandma being attacked by a big black bird!

CHAPTER 15

THE LITTLE CHURCH

When September showed up, we were still working on the same project on Dauphin Island. Being on a job for more than just a few weeks was (happily) new to us. The property had been transformed by now. We had cleared the land bare, burned all the huge pines and oak trees, and buried the stumps under what is today a tennis court. We would have gotten in a lot of trouble for doing that, but so many years have passed by now, and the court didn't sink, so I guess it doesn't matter anymore.

We used a couple of dragline cranes to excavate a big round-shaped hole, and then we drove down concrete sheet piling into a circular shape to create an artificial boat harbor. We used the old Caterpillar dozer to spread the sand we had dug out. Then we hooked up pile driving leads to our cranes and pounded wooden creosote pilings into the ground for the foundations for a bunch of small two-story houses that surrounded the artificial boat harbor.

The term *condos* was just now entering the American lexicon, and the owners would strut around like a bunch of turkeys as they proudly showed off the place to potential buyers.

We still had a few more months to go on the job. There was more piling to drive, piers to build, and drainage pipe to lay, which would take us right on into the new year. More importantly though, this condo project had given to Susan and me our first feeling of stability, and we were grateful for that.

Over the years, I have passed by the place probably several hundred times. I have even on occasion stopped and walked around the harbor. The last time I did, a security guard asked me what I was doing there. I told him about the work we had done there. He thought it was interesting, but he still told me that the place was private, and he politely asked me to leave. I smiled at him and said, "Sure, buddy, no problem."

Just for the record, the place is located on the northeast end of Dauphin Island, Alabama. It's just up the road from the Dauphin Island–to–Fort Morgan ferry landing. They named the place the Colony Cove Yacht Club, but to me it will always be "the place where Edgar came from."

Back then, Saturdays had lapsed into a routine of fixing up the yard in the morning, playing with Edgar all afternoon, and then after he roosted, sitting around the fire with Richard, Buck, and other friends. We'd roast some meat, and then poke at the coals till around ten o'clock, then we'd go inside and watch an incredibly funny new TV show called *Saturday Night Live*.

On the last Saturday night of September, Susan and I had a very serious discussion about church. We had gradually slipped out of the habit of going to church, or perhaps better put, slipped into the habit of not going at all. We had always gone to the Baptist church where Susan had grown up. The church was in Mobile, and due to Susan's "condition" it was becoming difficult for her to get ready in time to make the ride to Mobile and back. There was a newly established little Pentecostal church just up the road from us. I knew some of the people there and had heard that they were going to be "trying out" a new pastor that Sunday, so Susan and I decided that we would attend the eleven o'clock service to see if it might be a convenient place for us to worship.

I got up early morning. Susan was still waking me to coffee and breakfast. After eating, Susan went back to bed for her morning nap. I gathered up some food for Edgar, went outside, and watched him gulp it down. He still saved his precious piece of cheese for last. He wouldn't peck my eye anymore, so I would let him stay on me as long as he wanted. He could keep his balance with his wings no matter what I'd do. I could bend over or chop some brush, and he could stay right on my shoulder the whole time. At ten o'clock I brushed him off and went inside to shower and get dressed for church. At 10:55, I helped Susan into her car and we drove up to the church.

As we walked up the steps, we saw Edgar land in the small cedar tree that stood at the corner of the church. "Go back home," I said, but he sat there as we entered the sanctuary. I told Susan, "I bet he'll be waiting right there until church is over." I knew that Edgar had been on a few excursions since his battle for the earring, but as far as I knew, he hadn't been around any "other" people … until now.

We went inside and sat down near the back. They had already finished the Sunday school part and were about to begin the music ceremony. Several of the adult members that constituted their choir section had already lined up behind the rostrum. The reverend doubled as the music director. There were children scattered throughout the congregation because they didn't have a nursery or a children's service set up yet.

A couple of members sang a few special pieces and then the choir started up. It didn't take long for Susan and me to discover that when they start singing at a Pentecostal church, they take the "make a joyful noise to the Lord" part literally. There was a talented lady pounding on the piano ("Jerry Lee Lewis" style), and they had two tambourine players who seemed to be dueling. The guitar man was strumming with everything he had, although he couldn't be heard over the sound of the singing.

Everything was going just fine—folks were clapping their hands and having a real good time in general—when all of a sudden a big black crow landed on the windowsill right up toward the front pews and started pecking and banging away at the window. I don't know if it was the sound of the music, or if he was looking for Susan. I really think it was the latter. Perhaps he was just being a crazy crow! Whatever the reason, he would rap on that window for a while, then he would fly to the next window and rap on that one for a while, making his way from window to window.

The choir slowly began to fade out and then stopped altogether. Then came the children! One or two of them freaked out for a second, but for the most part, most of them thought it was delightful. Some of them escaped from their parents and ran to the window where Edgar was. They were laughing and clapping gleefully. A few little fellows were holding their noses up to the window. While Edgar kept pecking away, the parents had to get up from their seats or come down from the choir to round up their children. They were rounded up in an orderly way, except for one little guy who was probably about four. He had to be dragged by the arm, screaming all the way back to his seat. Some of the people already knew that we had a crow, but they hadn't seen him before now.

Most of the people were trying to smile as they still tried to subdue their kids. The older kids were laughing a bit, but you could hear the shrill sounds of "look at the bird," going off from various locations throughout the church. Then we realized that everybody in the place was half turned around, and they were looking at us. We looked up at the reverend … well, he wasn't smiling at all. I said out loud, "Oh man."

I got up, walked outside, and around to the side of the church. "Get outta here," I yelled as I approached Edgar. He didn't even turn around; he ignored me. He had stopped rapping on the window, but he was still looking in. I knocked him off the sill, and he flew up on the roof. "Please go home," I said with a hushed voice. He hopped along the roof like he was enjoying himself.

Then I noticed that the folks inside were looking out at me as I waved my arms. I walked back inside and sat down. Susan wasn't embarrassed at all. She was holding her mouth, suppressing a laugh! I thought to myself, *She's so cool. We come up here and disrupt the whole church, and she thinks it's funny.* That's when I copped an attitude. After all, it wasn't my fault; I didn't bang on the window.

Needless to say, the choir was over. The choir members filed down and took their seats in the pews. Then the reverend started his sermon. This guy started his sermon like a racehorse coming out of the gate. He was wide open from the get-go. I'm not going to lie; I'll tell you the truth ... I didn't like it. I didn't like his style, and I certainly didn't like what he was saying. He seemed to be mad at somebody, and I figured it must be me.

After only about five minutes in, Edgar landed on a window on the other side of the church. He didn't rap on the window. He was actually behaving himself rather well. The problem was though, that nobody was looking at the reverend. The place had neither curtains nor shades, and everyone was looking at Edgar. The reverend bellowed out, "Y'all look at me!"

I took that as the signal, and I said, "C'mon, Susan, let's go." She understood perfectly. We stood up and quietly walked out. As we drove away, I saw Edgar flying home. When we got home, Edgar landed on Susan's shoulder. We laughed all day. By the way, I heard that the congregation voted to get another preacher.

I need to point something out. I told this story about going to the little church that Sunday, not to make light or fun of the church nor the people. Quite the contrary. That little church holds a very special place in our hearts and memories. We visited the church many times and received innumerable blessings from the sermons, music, and the sweet-spirited people. I told the story because it happened, and also to point out the fact that Edgar had followed Susan's car. He hadn't done this before. It was another of those small series of events that would change things forever.

CHAPTER 16

THE BIRDS

You've probably noticed that we did a lot of laughing. Our baby was going into its eighth month, and we had gone through the whole time with nearly nonstop laughter. Through the years, laughter has been like the hallmark of our family, and we have had far more than our fair share of good times. Edgar taught us to laugh, even through the hard times.

The fact that Edgar would follow Susan's car gave cause for concern. I now knew that he had been leaving the property during the week. When I'd get home from work, twice he wasn't there waiting for me. When he'd finally get home, I'd scold him the way my dad used to do to me when I'd get home too late at night. Susan told me that he had followed her when she drove to visit my mom. I worried that he would fly to somebody's house and start clowning around and get shot or even worse, somebody might put him in a cage.

We went to have Sunday dinner with my mom and dad, and Edgar followed us over the car all the way there. My brothers, Russell, Richard, Sammy, and my little sister, Sarah, were there. My eighty-year-old grandaddy was there too. Edgar showed off and everyone had a grand ole time watching Richard and me play the air games with him.

My old grandaddy was particularly delighted to have Edgar land on his shoulder. My mom still has an old picture of that.

I didn't say anything to anyone about it, but I didn't like it that Edgar had flown so far from home. When we left to go home he followed us back, but a few hours later Mom called and said that Edgar was back at her house and was outside playing with my grandaddy. I didn't know what to do. There was nothing I could do, so I sat in my swing waiting for him to come to roost. He got home late. I didn't scold him; I was just glad to see him.

The next day when I got home, Susan had to rush off because someone was giving her a baby shower. I got home late and didn't see Edgar. That was bad, and I worried. I was still outside when Susan left. Just as it got dark I heard him flutter up to his roost. Looking up I said, "Trying to sneak in the window, ain't cha."

When Susan got home, I went outside to help her bring in her gifts. I made four or five trips, bringing in boxes of baby stuff. We stayed up till midnight looking at little tiny socks, bibs, rattles, and a bunch of stuff that I didn't know what it was. There were stacks of cloth diapers (there were no Huggies or Pampers back then). I know how silly I must have looked, putting tiny socks on my big toes and playing with baby stuff. Most of the clothes were white, because they didn't have machines to tell you the gender of your baby. Susan already had the nursery totally decked out with a baby bed and a curious windup machine that suspended little animal caricatures over the bed as it spun them around.

Susan and I were totally and completely happy! We were living in the halcyon days. We would talk late into the night about playing with our baby. By now I had turned the yard into a playground. All of this was so cool, but there was one variable that we discussed at length. How do you raise a child with a crazy wild crow? We had agreed that we would never turn our back on that child, because Edgar was so unpredictable.

Susan still called him, "Her sweet pretty bird," but me, I wasn't so sure. He acted different around each of us. She had seen his sweet side, while I had seen another side. He had definitely learned the child's game of playing one person off the other. He also developed an intense jealousy for Susan. Whenever Susan came outside, he was quick to leave me and go to her. When we sat together on the swing, he would invariably place himself between us. If we tried to do any snuggling, he would get green-eyed, and then squawk and squeeze in between our necks until he succeeded in separating us. If it took pecking me on the face or head to accomplish this, then so be it.

Susan thought this was so funny, but I thought I detected a bit of a mean streak in him, and I wondered what he might do when he saw Susan holding her baby. She thought I was just being paranoid, but again, I wasn't so sure.

The next event was prefaced by a media event. We didn't have cable TV in the country in those days. There may have been a few satellite disks. I can't really remember exactly when they became available, but when the first ones did come along, they were so big that they looked like an open parachute landing in the yard. Also, there were no VCRs at the time, so every now and then the TV networks would put on what they called a "major motion picture event." For a week, one of the three TV channels (I can't recall which one) had been announcing and playing it up big, that they were going to show the Alfred Hitchcock production of the movie, *The Birds*. When the movie finally aired, it naturally preempted the normal prime-time programs.

Everyone was talking about it. Susan and I hadn't seen the movie before, and we received calls all week from friends who knew about Edgar, telling us that this would be one of those "must see" movies. We waited with a thrilled anxiousness for the "big show." It may be hard to believe now, with all the blood and gore that has become commonplace on TV today, but at that time the movie was considered to be a horror movie, or at least a suspense thriller.

Richard and Brenda came over to watch the show with us. Susan made some popcorn, and we settled down and watched the movie. We considered it to have lived up to its billing. We didn't know much about special effects at the time and we wondered how Mr. Hitchcock could have gotten those birds to behave so viciously. Richard and I definitely related to the movie, remembering the way that Edgar's family and flock had swarmed around the bulldozer as I was taking down his nest tree. I remember Richard saying to Susan and Brenda, "I can see crows acting that way. They seem to flock together with a unity of purpose, but seagulls, no way; they just flock up because they're stupid."

Anyway, we enjoyed the movie all the more because we had Edgar. After the movie a few people phoned us to ask if we had watched the show. A lot of people had met Edgar by now, and I'm sure that each and every one of them had thought of him as they watched the movie.

You've learned that Edgar was constantly getting into something. It had become one thing after another. It had come to the point of us wondering what he was gonna do next, and when he was gonna do it. This time, it wouldn't take long at all.

The next event had a direct correlation to the movie that the whole of Mobile County had just watched. Sometimes Edgar could be slightly annoying, and sometimes he could be downright aggravating, but 99 percent of the time he was a bundle of fun and a joy to be around. I do admit however, that people like the woman with the one remaining long, shiny, dangly earring, would not think him funny at all. What happened next was not funny; as a matter of fact, it was bad.

A couple of nights after *The Birds* aired, Susan went to a Tupperware party. She brought home some pretty neat stuff. I didn't know what Tupperware was and I was enjoying making the containers burp, when Susan came and sat down next to me. She wasn't smiling, and I knew something was wrong. There was a new family that just the week before had moved a new house trailer in up on Jeffery Road, which was up the hill from our valley. They had a young teenage daughter. She had walked out the door the morning after the Hitchcock movie, and Edgar was sitting on the roof above the door. As she closed the door, Edgar let out one of his screams and flew toward her. I'm sure he didn't mean any harm, but she had no way of knowing that, and it scared the girl so bad that she fell backward off the porch.

Susan said, "There was a party at their house," and the girl had gotten banged up and injured real bad. She had cuts, scratches, and bruises all over her. Worse than that, she had a cast from her hip, down to her ankle. Sammy went to school with her and told me that she had actually broken her pelvis! He also told me that she had seen the movie the night before. Can you imagine waking up and walking outside right into a Hitchcock movie? That had to have been frightening! I felt terrible for the little girl. I wasn't angry with Edgar, but I heard that her daddy was. I was very concerned that somebody would eventually shoot Edgar. This was exactly the reason that I worried about him leaving the property.

When I went out for work Monday morning, he was waiting for me. I stroked him as he sat on my arm. He was a very big bird now. I didn't say much to him. He had been with us a long time—over eight months now. He was a full-grown adult bird. Something about him had changed though. I'd talk to him and he would slowly turn and look away. That hurt.

On the ride to Dauphin Island, I told Richard about the little girl getting hurt. He thought it was very funny. No, that's not quite right. He thought it to be hilarious. He would laugh uncontrollably, stop, bang on the top of the steering wheel, and laugh some more. When I expressed my regret over the matter, he would say (like always), "Aw, man, you need to tighten up." Then he'd say, "Serves 'em right."

You see, Richard was a little bit older than me. He had already gone through some heartrending events that had turned him to stone. No doubt about it, he was cold. We had grown up in those woods together, and we knew every inch of Peaceful Valley like the back of our hands, and Richard seemed to carry a morbid grudge toward anyone who had the audacity to move within a couple of miles of our valley. I'll just stop right there; it will take another book to explain.

CHAPTER 17

OIL AND WATER

Richard and I worked out the day and made the ride back home. I jumped out of the truck and started up the driveway. Edgar came flying out to meet me, which made me feel good. He landed on my arm and made his way up to my shoulder. I was every bit as glad to see him as I had been in what we had already started to call "back in the day." I hate to admit it, but as he became an adult, I had almost started to take him for granted. I vowed that I would never do that again. I was as proud as a peacock as I approached the porch.

I saw a little hole open in the curtains of the bedroom as I walked by. This had always been a comforting gesture to me that told me that Susan was inside and all was well. Edgar flew off my shoulder as I opened the back door to go into the kitchen. I sat my lunch bucket down and headed for Susan in the bedroom. I had always been met with the sound of "Did you have a nice day?" As I approached the hallway, I heard something altogether different. I heard the sound of weeping! My steps turned into a sprint to the bedroom. I was seeing and hearing something that I had never seen nor heard before.

Susan was sitting on the side of the bed crying. There was a puddle of tears on the floor that had splashed off her feet. I'd seen Susan shed a stray tear before, but I had never seen her sob. She looked up at me in pure anguish. My heart fell to my feet. My reflex reaction was one of sinking fear. "Our baby" was my first instinctive thought.

"What's wrong?" I said as I wrapped my arms around her.

"They're going to take our house away from us," she said as she wept.

I thought that I had heard her wrong or something, because those words didn't make any sense at all. They didn't even register. Holding her little shoulders with outstretched arms, I said, "What about the baby?" which proved to her that I hadn't heard what she said.

"They're going to take our home. This house trailer isn't ours," she said as her look became stern.

The only thing going through my head was that the baby was all right, and that something strange was wrong with Susan. She blinked away some tears and shook her head, and again, between sobs said, "They're going to take our home."

I sat beside her and took her in my arms and said, "Aw, sweetheart, it's okay." (By now, I was concerned about her mental stability.) "Ain't nobody gonna take our house. Who told you something crazy like that?"

She sobbed another time or two and said, "The FBI."

Now I was really concerned about her! I was still holding her when I said with a little chuckle, "Ha, the FBI. Don't you fret no more. Ain't nobody or nobody's army gonna take our house."

Then she shrugged her shoulders and twisted out of my arms, reached over to the nightstand, and picked up some official looking papers, which she handed to me. I paused as I looked at her curiously. Then unfolding the papers, I saw what I guess you call the official bonafide logo of the Federal Bureau of Investigation. I didn't start reading; I just sat there staring at the logo with a tunnel vision type of look.

"I don't believe it," I said. I'd never had a document like that in my hands before. "They've made a mistake," I said.

"Read it, go on and read it," she said. "You don't believe me, well read it!" She was still sobbing, but I could tell that she was perturbed at me by now.

I read the paper and then read it again. The legal jargon was befuddling. The "to whits," the "therefore this," the "therefore that," the "parties of this and that" parts were very hard to digest, but the gist of it was plain to see. These folks were saying that I might be involved in some kind of conspiracy and that I had willfully bought and attempted to conceal stolen property that had been transported from one state to another. I was dumbstruck to say the least.

I kept staring at the papers while Susan kept saying, "Well, what about it?"

"Where'd you get this?" I said. Susan told me about getting the knock on the door and the two FBI agents who were there when she opened it.

My shock turned into anger, and then rage. I thought of the man I had given the $4,000 to. How the trailer had almost magically appeared on my property that day. I thought how I'd borrowed the money to pay for it, worked so hard to set the house trailer up. I thought of the whole series of events. I thought until my brain ached.

Then came the question from Susan that I didn't have the answer for. "What are we going to do?" Now, this was the first time in my life, (it wouldn't be the last) that I had to reach down real hard and say, "Don't worry, everything will be all right." I probably could have won an Academy Award that night for pretending to be strong in the face of adversity. Susan had composed herself somewhat and seemed to take comfort in my unadulterated faking.

I gently grilled Susan on trying to remember exactly what the FBI agents had said. I tried to get a verbatim account, being careful not to upset her, which was practically impossible. The only thing she totally recalled was that they were going to take our house trailer and that one of the agents wanted to talk to me as soon as possible.

Needless to say, it was early the next morning before we fell asleep from mental exhaustion. I had walked around outside a couple of times that night and had privately destroyed a few things to vent my anger. I remember talking out loud to myself asking, "Okay, dude, whatcha gonna do now?" I didn't know. I woke up late the next morning. Susan was still asleep, and I didn't want to wake her. I was making some coffee when Richard knocked on the door. I opened the door and apologized for not being ready. I told him to go on ahead and that I would drive my old truck down later.

"You okay?" he said.

I answered, "I'll tell you about it later."

Susan was still asleep at eight o'clock. I didn't want to bother her, so I made my own breakfast, then made a sandwich for lunch and headed out to feed Edgar. I could already hear him calling before I opened the door to give him an extra piece of cheese and a lot of petting. I was absolutely torn up and didn't know what I was going to do about Edgar. I was so messed up that I was thinking what it would be like to live in a tent. Then I went back inside and woke Susan up with some coffee. We did a lot of hugging, but there wasn't much talking.

I rumbled on down to the island in my old Dodge truck. I was doing some layout for the piers we were about to build. I kept looking over my shoulder at the entrance road. I was tired and depressed. My mind kept wandering away with every bad scenario possible. One time, I'd be telling myself that I shouldn't be here. I should be at home protecting Susan from the evil federals, and then a minute later I would imagine being surrounded by a bunch of G-men, guns drawn and all.

I couldn't stop my brain. I remember looking at my watch at eleven o'clock when I saw a man standing in front of the condo office talking to an owner. This guy was wearing a dark suit, and he had on a pair of dark sunglasses. I'd seen a lot of people with suits talking to the owners before, and I was just about to dismiss my anxiety, when the owner pointed in my direction and made a sweeping gesture from his face to his chest, like he was imitating my beard. The two of them shook hands and the man in the suit started walking toward me.

"Well, this is it," I told myself. As he drew nearer, I started walking to meet him. He did the old routine where he opened his wallet and showed me his badge. Then he asked me how I had come into possession of the house trailer. He was a real down-to-business, no-fooling-around type of guy.

I resorted to something that would serve me well throughout my life: I told him the truth. I told him everything from meeting the man, to unexpectedly finding the house trailer on my land, borrowing the money to pay for it, even fixing up my yard in expectation of a new baby. He turned out to be one of the nicest fellows I've ever met. He assured me that he would put in a good word for me and see to it that I wouldn't be held accountable for the crime. The man told me that I probably wouldn't even have to go to court.

I was informed that the trailer man was already in custody, and how they had caught the man's truck driver, and how he had ratted everyone out. The agent even told me that I had a lovely wife. He also told me that I would have to surrender the evidence, but they were going to allow us to stay in the house trailer until after the baby was born, and for that I was grateful. All in all, he made me feel a lot better. Oh sure, I was still in a pretty bad spot, but at least I now knew that I didn't have to worry about going to prison.

We had finished talking and had shaken hands when he said a cool thing. Before he turned to walk away, he asked, "Oh, by the way, did you know there's a big crow flying around your place?"

I said, "Yep, sure do."

The relief that I had gained from talking to the agent was short-lived. I was indeed beholding to him for his kindness and understanding, but soon it began to seem like everything I looked at had a sign on it saying, "What are you going to do next?" I had already figured out that I had a few housing options open to me, but all of them included having to move away from my beloved valley, even if just temporarily.

The question of what to do about Edgar was like a mixture of anger and heartbreak, which don't mix very well. If you take a jar and pour in some water and then some oil, you can shake it up and it will turn into a cloudy, ugly liquid. After a while the two substances will separate and the oil will wind up on top. If you mix and shake up anger and heartbreak, the same thing happens. After a while the anger will wind up on top. For the next few weeks, I shook that jar pretty hard.

When I'd get home, Susan would be sitting on the swing waiting for me. This was out of the ordinary for her. I would put my arm around her, while she laid her head on my shoulder. Naturally, Edgar would be there with her, and I know that he knew that something was wrong. All the pranks and funny antics were over now. The three of us would gently swing back and forth. Edgar was also a big part of the equation that we couldn't find an answer for. What would become of him was almost too terrible to think of. Susan and I were under what would turn out to be a delusion that he couldn't survive without us.

The next week passed, and Susan and I were treating the situation like snakes in the swamp. Every good coon hunter knows what I mean. You know there are snakes in the swamp, but if you want to get from here to there, you have to just start walking. You don't look to the left or to the right; you have to keep going straight ahead.

CHAPTER 18

TWINKLES IN HER EYES

When Saturday morning came, I walked outside and something absolutely incredible was happening. A totally unexpected event; one of those series of events that started with an advertisement in a newspaper, and believe me, it caught me completely off guard.

Crows!

For the very first time in over eight months, I heard the raucous sound of a big flock of crows! I ran to the front yard and looking toward the huge pines that covered the north hillside, I saw the biggest flock of crows that I had ever seen. They completely blacked out the green tops that were less than a hundred yards away—and they were screaming their heads off! They were hopping and flapping and leap-frogging over each other.

Before I met Edgar, I thought that crows were crazy, mindless, and comical creatures, flying around almost bumping into each other … Nevermore. I now knew that I was looking at a flock of highly intelligent, cunning birds.

Edgar was screaming back from the top of an oak tree. I then noticed something peculiar and puzzling. All the flock of crows and Edgar too, were in a crouching, leaning, pointing posture. The entire flock seemed to be aiming themselves at Edgar, and Edgar was aiming back. So much screaming and posturing was going on that I assumed that the flock was preparing to attack Edgar and that he was in a defensive stance.

It quickly came to my mind that Edgar hadn't behaved in this manner since seeing himself in the mirror on Philip Brook's scooter. Not knowing what I was seeing or what I needed to do, I let out a rather feeble, "Hey, hey, Edgar."

Realizing that I couldn't be heard over the flocks' deafening din, I yelled as loud as I could, "Heeeay, Eeedgaaar!" At this the flock started rising up and coming back down again. They resembled a disorganized human wave at a football game! The racket died down for a few seconds and then rapidly rose into an astounding crescendo of *caw*s. Edgar turned his head and gave me a look, and then joined in with the chorus of crows.

Now I was really puzzled. I thought, *I wonder what's going on?* I was standing there stupefied when Edgar left the tree and glided down to me. When Edgar landed on my arm, I heard a very weird sound. The flock became almost silent. They were making what I can only describe as little, almost inaudible squeaking noises, and I promise, I could almost hear the crows saying, "Don't trust the human!"

As Edgar sat on my arm, he would look at me, then toward the house, and then toward the flock, and again, to me, the house, and the flock. He repeated this several times. I noticed that his claws were gripping me tighter than usual. I could tell that he was being torn. I believe, or rather I know that he kept looking toward the house because he knew that Susan was in there. With this, he lifted off my arm. I still, vividly remember what it felt like when his weight left my arm.

Edgar flew to the top of a pine that was about a hundred feet away from the flock. I have never to this day read up on crows. I don't know if they have a pecking order. I don't know if they have alpha males or females. I don't know if they have colonels or generals, but I'll tell you what I saw.

A dozen or so of the crows, acting as if they were the representatives of the flock, flew over to Edgar. I held my breath. Edgar and the "representatives," began to sort of nuzzle and seemed to be smelling each other. This examination lasted for about a minute. Then, together they all flew over into the middle part of the flock. Edgar was by far the largest crow in the flock. He was half again bigger than the others, and you could easily pick him out among the rest.

The cawing now peaked to its loudest. Then, as if someone had given a signal, the flock picked up and made a huge circle that encompassed the whole yard. I was awestruck! It was as if a big black swirling tornado had just sucked up our Edgar! My knees became weak and I had to lean against a tree as I watched them rapidly disappear toward the east. As they flew toward Big Creek Lake, the *caw*s became fainter until, just like that, Edgar was gone, and that was that. It all happened so fast—too fast. From the time that I had run into the front yard, to the time that the *caw*s had faded away had only taken five or six minutes.

I stood in that one spot, staring at the treetops for about an hour. My thoughts went in circles, up and down, from side to side. I had just witnessed a phenomenon! I know what I saw, and I don't know what I saw! My thoughts turned into memories. I went through the past eight months in a flash. After such a long time together, he simply flew away. I was at a loss. I thought what had just happened wasn't right, but then again, it was perfectly right.

When I went inside and numbly told Susan what had happened and that Edgar had gone, I saw her stiffen a bit. She paused, and then stoically and wisely replied as if reading from a script. "Well, that's what you always wanted isn't it, to give him his freedom? Now he's got it." She turned and walked away for a moment. When she came back, I could see where she had wiped away some tears.

I helped her outside and pointed out where the flock had been. I showed her the oak tree where Edgar had been confronting the flock. Waving my arms in sweeping circles, I tried to show her where the black vortex had tracked. She was amazing. She stood there silently for a while. Even though she didn't utter a word, the wet twinkles in her eyes told me all that I needed to know.

Susan and I spent the whole day truly alone for the first time in a long while. We sat in somber silence out in the now wearing-out swing. We hugged and smiled a lot. We even cried together. Then came what we called Edgar's glorious stage. After moping around that day and night thinking that we would never see him again, the next day he surprised us yet again.

We woke up and had a pleasant morning together. Susan made me a breakfast fit for a king. She was the Rock of Gibraltar now. She had turned the tables on me. Now, she was the one saying that everything would be all right. Ever since our first week of marriage, I had made it a point of giving her all the money I made. She was the official secretary-treasurer of our family. She had done some ciphering over the past few days and had come to realize that we had achieved the key to the Great American Dream.

We had real good credit and had stashed away plenty of savings for a sizable down payment for a house. I told her that if she found a house that she wanted, I would certainly buy it for her. We had actually become hopeful—maybe not optimistic yet, but we were working on it. (We would later find out that buying a house was easier than we thought, and we did it!)

I drove to the store and bought a newspaper. When I got home, it was so pleasant outside that I opened a few windows. I sat beside one of the open windows to peruse the classified section for a nice house. I had no sooner started, when outside I thought I heard the distant sound of cawing crows. I froze as I stared at the paper.

I was asking myself, "Did I just hear what I thought I heard?" Slowly I laid the paper down, reached over, and pulled the curtain back. I sat there listening and looking. I didn't hear anything. I was in the middle of telling myself, "You're just imagining things, you're just hoping too hard," when sure enough, clear as a bell, I heard the sound, not of crows, but the sound of a single crow.

I ran to the front door, threw it open, and without even bothering to use the steps, jumped and landed in the front yard. I scanned the treetops to the north, then the east, and then to the south. I couldn't tell where the *caw* was coming from, and I was trying to swallow my racing heart back down out of my throat. The sound seemed to hover over the valley, with a piece or two falling down to my ears. It sounded like music to me. I could very well tell that it was Edgar.

I wanted to shout, "Hey, Edgar!" Instead I jumped to the top of the steps and yelled, "Susan … Susan … come here, I hear Edgar!" I heard her say, "What?" It was one of those "whats," that mean, "I heard and understood what you said, but I can't think of any other way to answer because what you said excited me!"

She came shuffling into the living room. You see, this was the first Sunday in November, and the middle of November had been pronounced as her due date. Bless her heart, she looked and walked as if she was just about to burst. (Little did we know at the time that the little fellow inside her had already picked up his shovel and was contemplating which way to go in order to burrow himself out of there.)

Anyway, I helped Susan down the steps and into the front yard. Now, I know that Edgar had learned to like me, but with Susan it was different. From the first time that she had dropped that little dab of grits in his mouth, he had fallen absolutely, silly, goo-goo in love with her. Way back when he had been sticking tiny pieces of cheese into her blanket and rolling his eyes into the back of his head, making those weird cooing noises while she stroked him with her finger, I would think, "This ain't normal; this bird ain't right."

I finally zeroed in on Edgar's call. It was coming from the ridge to the south. The treetops on the ridge weren't visible from our vantage point. I hadn't called for him at all, but we realized from his calls that he was on his way. He appeared as he skimmed over the large bay trees that lined the swamp bottom. I heard Susan as she whispered, "Pretty bird." Edgar was winging his way to us with strong, slow flaps of his wings.

I saw that Susan had already turned her engagement ring down to the bottom side of her finger. I held out my arm as he approached, but he flew straight to Susan's shoulder. She slid her hand under him and held him out in front of her. She baby-talked him and called him, "Pretty bird." You could tell that he still loved her, but this time there was no cooing. He stood on the back of her hand straighter and taller than ever before. He seemed to be almost stretching himself to show his pride.

When I held out my hand to him, Edgar hesitated before hopping on. While on my arm, Susan started stroking him and rubbing his neck. He slowly raised his magnificent jet-black wings until they were perfectly horizontal. This he had never done before, and it was a breathtaking display. I could only utter, "whoa." He hopped back to Susan's arm and resumed his tall, proud stance. Susan and I stood in the yard like a couple of very proud parents. We were practically giddy in our joy and pride! This went on for a few minutes, when we heard the sound of other crows.

There, to the north side of our yard, in the same pine tops as the day before, crows started landing and cawing. At first there were just a few, and then small groups, then larger and larger groups until the tops were seething with crows! The crows were cawing, but compared to yesterday, they sounded almost timid. Then Edgar began glancing back and forth from Susan to the crows in quick jerks. He didn't even look at me, but I didn't care; I was just glad to be there.

Edgar had done many strange, weird, crazy, and funny things before, but it was like he was saving this one for last. He turned toward the crows and assumed the crouching, pointing posture of yesterday, and then he started cawing with all his might. We had never heard him that loud before. At this, the entire flock began the same crouching and pointing, with a cawing that sounded like a single, huge black crow! Edgar was nonstop cawing, and the flock was nonstop cawing back. It was almost intimidating!

Susan said, "Sounds like they're laughing at us."

I replied, "Kinda like *The Birds* movie, ain't it?" We still don't know what was going on. Perhaps they really were laughing at us poor, earthbound humans. Perhaps they were telling Edgar, "You shouldn't trust humans." We just don't know.

We were hoping that Edgar would spend some time with us, but we could see that this didn't fit well with our plans. Then, Edgar lifted off Susan's hand and joined his new family. Just like yesterday, we easily picked him out as he made his rounds through the flock because he was so large.

I said, "Maybe Island crows are bigger."

Susan replied, "Maybe so. I didn't know that until now, since we have other crows to compare him to. But maybe it's because he always had so much to eat."

Then we learned still another thing about Edgar. We really never exactly knew that he was a male crow. We just called him a "he" because it seemed to fit. As he made his "rounds" through the flock, he kept returning to a certain place each time. Susan saw it first. As the flock would separate to allow him to return to this place, she grabbed my arm while pointing and whispered excitingly, "Look. Oh my goodness, he's got a girlfriend!"

As it turned out, Edger had apparently already picked out a mate for himself. Edger and the little lady crow would almost snuggle as they flapped and cawed together, and then he would muscle his way through the mass of birds to do some of his aerobatic maneuvers before returning to his new sweetheart.

I said, "That's our boy. He's showing off for her."

Susan hugged me and said, "That is so sweet! Look at him. He seems to be so happy, doesn't he?"

With a lump in my throat, I could only answer, "Yeah, he does."

Still hugging, she looked up to me and said softly, "We did good, didn't we?"

Again, I could only say, "Yeah, we did."

We watched like proud parents to see that Edgar was already "King of the Canopy." The flock stayed long enough for us to see that he had assumed for himself a dominant position in the flock. Eventually Edgar and the flock flew away. We knew that we were just being sentimental, but to us the fading *caw, caw, caw*s sounded more like bye, bye, byes.

The rest of the afternoon was spent in reminiscent laughter and tears. Susan finally went back inside for her well-deserved rest. I stayed outside visiting with Richard. He had observed what he called the "crow show" from his hillside and had been standing directly under their exit.

He said, "They looked like a big swarm of locust." He and Edgar had been tight from the beginning, and the two of us would have many, "Remember what Edgar did," laughs throughout the years.

We heard the big flock echoing through the woods a few times that evening, but they never showed themselves. After building a fire, Richard and I just sat around under Edgar's roost, hoping against hope that he might show up one more time. He didn't. As the sun set, Richard got up to go. He said, "Well, I guess he's gone." I didn't answer; I just nodded my head.

I remember one time, years later when Susan had rented a Walt Disney movie about a little elephant with big ears. The little elephant's name was Dumbo. He had accidentally gotten "messed up" and woke up with a couple of crows above him. I laughed so hard because the crows reminded me of Edgar and Paul's cigarette. After the movie, I took it over to Richard's house and fast-forwarded it to the crow scene. We watched and rewound it maybe a dozen times. We laughed our heads off each time.

CHAPTER 19

FINAL FAREWELL

We had lost Edgar. I always knew that he'd leave someday, but I hoped he wouldn't. Strange thing though, as Susan and I talked about it that night, we were definitely glad for him. I always thought of his leaving with a sad foreboding because I imagined him getting shot or worse—being caged. He had gone and there was no more crying, only happiness.

Edgar had his own family now, and we were glad for him. Susan and I had raised a child crow into an adult crow. We had watched him leave into the world on his own, to begin a life with a family of his own. Susan and I would go on to have four children, and we had just learned many valuable lessons about life that would serve us well.

The ride to and from work the next week became different. Richard and I didn't talk and laugh as much. It was my fault because my thoughts and conversations were focused on Susan and the baby now. It may sound bad, but it's true. The little fellow in there had seemed like an abstract object to me. Now the reality of fatherhood was bearing down hard. I really don't know how to put it. Susan had turned into a loving mother the moment she found herself expecting. She had taken prenatal care to an extreme that was above and beyond the norm. She hadn't even drank a Coca-Cola for over eight months!

I had become a man in thought and deed, but the reality of fatherhood didn't truly hit me until that Sunday night after Edgar had left. Late that night Susan woke me up saying, "Wake up. Feel my stomach and look at this!" I quickly shook off the slumber and laid my hand on her stomach. We had fun feeling the baby move around before, but it had been nothing like this. He was thrashing about and kicking around. I remember saying, "Feels like it's trying to break out!"

Susan looked a little uncomfortable, but her smile was glowing like a floodlight. Then, (this was the thing that really got to me) I watched with openmouthed amazement as a lump appeared on one side of her stomach and then moved across slowly to the other side. Susan was giggling with wide-eyed delight as the lump came up, moved to the other side, and disappeared. Then it would reemerged down lower and track across her skin. It was wonderful and astounding.

Edgar had given me some "candid moments" before, but this little baby had already, without even being born, totally eclipsed, outdone, and outshown by far anything that Edgar had ever done! Edgar had entered into that dreamland of memory, but we knew that his place was about to be more than taken.

Every night that week, when the baby would move, I would cup my hands on Susan's stomach and talk to the baby in a low, soft voice, the same low voice that had calmed Edgar when he had been young. Susan said that we had two or more weeks to go, so I wanted the baby to know my voice and recognize me as soon as he was born. We didn't know if such a thing was even possible, but we thought it wouldn't hurt to try.

That Friday evening, I was anxious to get home. It had been cold and windy all day, and I was looking forward to a nice warm weekend with Susan. As I got out of the truck, I told Richard that I might start driving my old Dodge truck to work next week, just in case I had to unexpectedly go to the hospital.

It was dark and getting colder outside as I made my way up the driveway. I was walking fast because I wanted to get inside to warm up. I approached the porch and had started untying my boot laces when

Susan's voice startled me. I heard her say, "Have a nice day?" It wasn't really her voice that startled me, but the direction from which it came.

I popped up like a jack-in-the-box and spun around in my tracks. It took me a couple of seconds to make out her silhouette. She was standing in the front yard, hidden by the dark shadow of a big oak tree. I walked toward her and said, "What are you doing out here? Are you all right?" Then, "Are you crazy? Don't you know it's too cold out here for you?"

As I joined her in that dark place in the yard, she beamed a smile and said, "Edgar came to see me; you just missed him."

I think I already knew she was going to say that by reading her smile. My disappointment of having missed him was tempered by her pleasure of having seen him. I asked, "How was he, and how long was he here?"

She said, "He was just fine, but something about him looked different. He looked bigger and stronger and more handsome than ever." She went on to explain that he hadn't come down to her arm. Susan pointed to a low limb and said, "I heard him call to me, so I walked over here and found him standing right there on that limb. I talked to him and held out my arm. I thought he was about to come to me, but when you got out of Richard's truck, he flew away when you shut the door."

I tried not to let it show, but that made me feel real bad. I must have looked a bit pitiful though because she put her arm around my waist and layed her head on my shoulder. She said, "Oh, I'm sorry."

That's when something occurred to me. I turned and put both my hands on her shoulders and said, "What were you doing out here anyway?"

Susan answered, "I was inside getting supper ready, and for some reason I started feeling really warm. A few seconds later I got hot, so I opened the door to get some cool air and as soon as I did, that's when I heard Edgar, so I came out to find him."

"Okay," I said, "but are you all right?"

She said, "Oh yeah, I'm fine, except now I'm cold. Let's go inside."

I took a nice hot bath, while Susan prepared my favorite Friday night meal: chili dogs. We had a wonderfully ordinary Friday night. We watched TV and talked some about Edgar, but mostly about our baby. There was no talk about losing our house or any related plans. We were ignoring that because we thought we still had some time left to deal with it. After all, they had told us that we could stay until after the baby arrived, so we decided not to worry about it anymore until then. We were still so happy. We stayed up till almost midnight, and then went to the bedroom.

As we lay down, Susan made the comment, "The baby is moving around a lot. My stomach feels kinda hard, and it seems to be lower." We thought nothing of it.

All that evening I had kept my thoughts about Edgar to myself. As I closed my eyes, I was still bummed out about not seeing him that evening, and especially about how he had flown away just as I got home. As I drifted off to sleep, my thoughts were with him.

The last of those events that would change everything forever now unexpectedly rushed into place. About seven hours later, our first male child was born, and the most dramatic turning point in my life had happened. This was different than a bird; this was a human being. We named our boy Daniel. Then later came our next boy, Ab, who was followed by Lucas. It's amazing how each one is just as special as the other!

Many times, such as when they each took their first walk across the room, or when they did some of their funny antics, or even when they did something that might get them in trouble, I would get an eerie feeling like, "I've been here before."

Like any proud parent, I'm naturally inclined to start telling you stories about our boys and how their behaviors would parallel those of Edgar's, which were all too obvious. I'll have to restrain myself though because this was a story about a bird and the woman he loved. The boys … maybe next time.

Our last child was my beautiful daughter, Allison. She didn't remind me of a crazy crow the way my sons did … with one slight exception.

She was a precious baby. She didn't go through the terrible twos, but oh boy, she was a "ferocious four"! She was definitely a mama's girl. When Susan and I sat together, she'd scream, "No, no; that's my mama!" She'd climb up and wedge her little body between us. If I tried to reach around her to pull them both into a hug, she would hit me with her soft tiny hand. Like Edgar, she was madly jealous of Susan. Déjà vu again.

I believe in the providence of God, and I believe in divine timing. I truly believe that the Lord sent me a very unusual animal to raise to help teach me many lessons about children and life.

I think it's all about getting ready for freedom and not being caged. Eventually they will live their own lives. Parents know what it's like. When your kids take their first steps, they're walking away from you. When they learn to pedal a tricycle, they're riding away from you. When you drop them off at the first grade, they're forming their own world. When they grow up, you become a memory. Be careful what kind of memory you become.

There are so many—perhaps too many—lessons to learn. Here is one of the most important lessons of all: When God gives you children to care for and raise, remember that you're not raising boys or girls; you're raising men and women.

I ended this narrative of Edgar fast, because it ended fast. Amazingly we saw Edgar one more time. One day as we were hauling away our belongings to our new house, we saw a flock of crows on top of some pines near a lake that Richard and I built up on County Road 5. Seeing a crow that was so much bigger than the rest, we stopped the truck and got out. The large crow flew down and landed on a nearby limb.

I said, "Hey, Edgar, how you been?" He turned his head from side to side and cawed! He raised his magnificent black wings and cawed again. We about broke our faces smiling. He rejoined his flock and flew away. We never saw him again with our eyes, although we can still see him in our memories.

I'm an old man now; my red beard has turned white. For the past thirty-seven years I have never seen a crow without thinking about Edgar. Sometimes, I even hold out my arm and yell, "hey." For several years after he left, in the valley I would see some crows that were bigger than the others, and I always liked to think that perhaps, they might be Edgar's descendants.

Oh, just for the record, everything concerning our housing arrangements turned out just fine. And one more thing. After writing the story of Edgar, my dad passed away. After the funeral, Susan walked up to me and pointed out a pretty lady. She told me that this was the little girl that Edgar had caused to fall off the porch after *The Birds* movie—the same girl who had all the cuts and bruises at the Tupperware party. I didn't know her, but she knew who I was. She told me all about the incident—and that she actually had broken her hip. She laughed about the whole thing; after all, it was many years ago.

Soon everybody around was laughing. It was a cool situation. It occurred to me, that after all those years, Edgar was still making people laugh! I asked her if I could use her name. She said, "Of course." Her name is Teresa Childers, and by the way, she told me that her dad would have definitely shot Edgar if given a chance. (Which is exactly why I used to worry about him when he started leaving the property.)

AUTHOR BIO

Moses enjoys restoring and operating heavy construction equipment. Old cranes are his forte. He is an avid reader of histories and biographies. Moses and his wife Susan live in Mobile, Alabama. They have four children, and eight grandchildren.